A KIDS' GUIDE TO

AMERICA'S
BILL OF RIGHTS

A KIDS' GUIDE TO

AMERICA'S
BILL OF RIGHTS

REVISED
AND
UPDATED
EDITION

KATHLEEN KRULL

★ ILLUSTRATED BY ANNA DIVITO ★

HARPER

An Imprint of HarperCollinsPublishers

Library of Congress Cataloging-in-Publication Data
Krull, Kathleen.
    A kids' guide to America's Bill of Rights : curfews, censorship, and the 100-pound
giant / by Kathleen Krull ; illustrated by Anna DiVito.
        p.   cm.
    Includes bibliographical references and index.
Summary: Examines the ten amendments to the United States Constitution that make
up the Bill of Rights, explaining what the amendments mean, how they have been
applied, and the rights they guarantee.
    ISBN 978-0-06-235231-6 (trade) — ISBN 978-0-06-235230-9 (pbk.)
    1. United States Constitution 1st–10th Amendments—Juvenile literature.
2. Constitutional amendments—United States. 3. Civil rights—United States—
Juvenile literature. [1. United States, Constitution. 1st–10th Amendments.
2. Constitutional amendments. 3. Civil rights.] I. DiVito, Anna, ill. II. Title.
KF4750 .K78 1999   99-17324
342.73'085—dc21   CIP
                                                                             AC

Typography by Chelsea C. Donaldson
23 24 25 26 27 LBC 12 11 10 9 8
❖
First HarperCollins Publishers Printing, 1999
Second Edition

To Colin Krull, in honor of fireworks, root beer floats,
and your career in law

—K.K.

To Joseph and Jonathan

—A.D.

CONTENTS

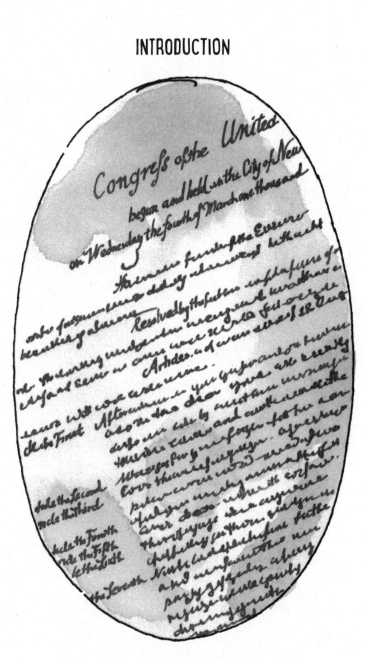

The Bill of Rights—What Is It?

The list we call the Bill of Rights may *seem* simple. After all, it's only 462 words long. But since it became law over 200 years ago—in 1791—millions of words have been written about it. And a lot of those words affect the way you live every day.

QUESTION: What is the Bill of Rights?
SIMPLE ANSWER: The first ten amendments (or additions) to the United States Constitution.

QUESTION: What is its point?
SIMPLE ANSWER: To protect people against government.

Congratulations. You now know something many grown-ups do not. In one survey, 33 percent of *adults* couldn't identify the Bill of Rights, and fewer than 10 percent knew its purpose. Numbers like these make some people panic: Is the Bill of Rights in danger of being forgotten?

But the Bill of Rights won't be forgotten by those who realize it's about important stuff—sometimes even life-and-death stuff. It's a list of ten promises intended to protect the rights of all Americans—including kids.

Because of it, the federal (or national) government cannot tell you what to believe, or what to say, or what religion to practice, or what friends you can have.

That makes the Bill of Rights the broadest protection of individual freedom ever written.

Here They Are—the 462 Words

These are the very important words of the United States Bill of Rights:

1. Congress shall make no law respecting an establishment of religion, or prohibiting the free exercise thereof; or abridging the freedom of speech, or of the press; or the right of the people peaceably to assemble, and to petition the Government for a redress of grievances.

2. A well regulated Militia, being necessary to the security of a free State, the right of the people to keep and bear Arms, shall not be infringed.

3. No Soldier shall, in time of peace be quartered in any house, without the consent of the Owner, nor in time of war, but in a manner to be prescribed by law.

4. The right of the people to be secure in their persons, houses, papers, and effects, against unreasonable searches and seizures, shall not be violated, and no Warrants shall issue, but upon probable cause, supported by Oath or affirmation, and particularly describing the place to be searched, and the persons or things to be seized.

5. No person shall be held to answer for a capital, or otherwise infamous crime, unless on a presentment or indictment of a Grand Jury, except in cases arising in the land or naval forces, or in the Militia, when in actual service in time of War or public danger; nor shall any person be subject for the same offence to be twice put in jeopardy of life or limb; nor shall be compelled in any criminal case to be a witness against himself, nor be deprived of life, liberty, or property, without due process of law; nor shall private property be taken for public use, without just compensation.

6. In all criminal prosecutions, the accused shall enjoy the right to a speedy and public trial, by an impartial jury of the State and district wherein the crime shall have been committed, which district shall have been previously ascertained by law, and to be informed of the nature and cause of the accusation; to be confronted with the witnesses against him; to have compulsory process for obtaining witnesses in his favor, and to have the Assistance of Counsel for his defence.

7. In Suits at common law, where the value in controversy shall exceed twenty dollars, the right of trial by jury shall be preserved, and no fact tried by jury shall be otherwise re-examined in any Court of the United States, than according to the rules of the common law.

8. Excessive bail shall not be required, nor excessive fines imposed, nor cruel and unusual punishments inflicted.

9. The enumeration in the Constitution, of certain rights, shall not be construed to deny or disparage others retained by the people.

10. The powers not delegated to the United States by the Constitution, nor prohibited by it to the States, are reserved to the States respectively, or to the people.

CHAPTER 1

The Bill of Rights and You

★ ★ ★

These ten very important promises are part of the ultimate laws of the land—the guidelines all newer laws are supposed to respect.

QUESTION: What does all this gobbledegook really mean?

ANOTHER QUESTION: And what does the Bill of Rights mean to *you*?

Mysterious Things

AND A THIRD QUESTION: Why wasn't the Constitution enough?

You recall the Constitution. It's that very important document that spells out how the United States is to be governed.

TOP NINE THINGS TO REMEMBER ABOUT THE CONSTITUTION

1. It begins with "We the people."
2. It says that the majority of the people, through democratically elected representatives, govern the country.
3. It was drawn up in 1787 and went into effect two years later.
4. It sets up a balance between national (or federal) government and state governments.
5. It further separates powers by establishing three branches of national government: the executive (the president), the legislative (the Congress), and the judicial (the Supreme Court).

6. These branches of government check up on each other in a system of checks and balances, so no one branch gets too powerful.
7. No law can be passed that disagrees with it.
8. A lot of arguing went into the making of it.
9. A lot of arguing has gone on about it ever since.

★   ★   ★   ★   ★   ★   ★   ★   ★   ★

One of the beauties of our Constitution is its flexibility: it was built to last. In fact, its meaning changes with the times. It can even mean totally opposite things at different points in history. For example, in an 1896 Supreme Court case called *Plessy v.* [short for versus] *Ferguson*, racial segregation was found constitutional, which means OK according to the Constitution. But as of 1954, in another case called *Brown v. Board of Education*, the Court decided exactly the opposite: segregation was *un*constitutional, and therefore it was outlawed.

But no sooner was the Constitution wrestled into words than the mysteries and complications began. All sorts of people criticized it for all sorts of reasons. The general public's sorest spot was the Constitution's lack of a bill of rights. Having branches of government check on each other was nifty, but it wasn't enough. Minorities needed protection from the majority. Individual *people* needed protection from the *government*.

These critics argued that a powerful central government without safeguards for people was dangerous. Why? Because historically governments try to expand their power at the expense of individual liberty. We take such liberty for granted now, but back then American people suffered a lot of abuse without it. One critic actually compared a constitution lacking a bill of rights to arsenic that would poison your body; another called government a runaway horse that would break people's necks. One particularly violent critic said that he would rather chop off his right hand than sign a constitution without a bill of rights.

Early Americans compared the government to a dangerous runaway horse.

As it turned out, only because of pledges to add to it was the Constitution even ratified (or formally approved). Public opinion was loud and clear: the Constitution lacked a certain something.

The True Story of the Bill of Rights

The man of the hour in this story is James Madison. This congressman from Virginia had been an especially active participant in all the arguments about—and creation of—the Constitution.

Madison wrote the first draft of the Bill of Rights in 1789 and made it his business to get it accepted. He didn't invent the ideas in it—the Bill of Rights represented the summing up of decades of revolutionary thought. Instead, Madison borrowed things here and there, from

• various states' constitutions;

• sources such as England's Magna Carta—a document approved by King John in 1215, which protected people against royal abuses of power;

• his fellow Virginian George Mason, who had written Virginia's Declaration of Rights.

Madison's life was not easy. Despite public support for a bill of rights, most politicians were either indifferent or else actively hostile to his pet project. It took him two and a half *years* of debates—and, frankly, badgering his fellow congressmen—before he got the necessary agreement from the majority of states.

★ ★ ★ ★ ★ ★ ★ ★ ★ ★

THE 100-POUND GIANT

For his persistence with the Bill of Rights, James Madison will forever be known as its "father." But while shepherding it through the political process, Madison had a number of things working against him. One was his own doubt. He thought there were probably more urgent issues around. Privately he was skeptical about its value and was even known to refer to it as "a nauseous project." As ill as it might have made him, Madison saw the Bill of Rights as a way to increase his popularity with the public. He used it as a campaign issue in his close race against James Monroe for election to the first House of Representatives.

Another problem was Madison himself. He made a very poor first impression and had to work hard to overcome it. He was short and weighed just one hundred pounds. He was sickly, nervous, and shy, with such a weak voice that listeners often could not hear him. He delayed decisions as long as possible, so many people found him timid and indecisive.

Madison *was* smart. He had graduated from college in two years and then gone into politics. He also had a "secret weapon" in his wife, the energetic and enormously popular Dolley Madison. As an active delegate to the Constitutional Convention in 1787, Madison was the only one who thought to take notes (thus providing our only record of how the Constitution came to be written). The wife of one of the other delegates called Madison a "gloomy stiff creature," but others were kinder. Thomas Jefferson said that he knew of no man in all of America and Europe with more integrity or with "an abler head" than Madison.

Madison won that election against Monroe, and more elections later. Eventually, in 1809, he became the fourth president of the United States.

Dolley Madison. James Madison's influential wife.

And if you ever come into possession of a $5,000 bill, you will see on it a portrait of this giant of American legal history.

After the Bill of Rights was drafted, eleven states had to approve it to make it part of the Constitution. Georgia, Connecticut, and Massachusetts took no official action at the time, but nine other states (Delaware, Maryland, New Hampshire, New Jersey, New York, North Carolina,

Pennsylvania, Rhode Island, and South Carolina) fell into line within six months. Then Vermont joined the Union and added its endorsement.

Finally, on December 15, 1791, Virginia gave the go-ahead and became that crucial eleventh state. The Bill of Rights was now law, four years after the Constitution had been adopted.

Still Controversial After All These Years

The 462 words of the Bill of Rights celebrate America as a nation of individuals. They emphasize the tradition in the United States of expecting one's rights, of loving liberty above all else, and of distrusting authority. All people weren't equal in 1791—most African Americans were still slaves, all women were second-class citizens, the rich had more power than the poor—but the Bill of Rights laid the groundwork for equality to become a reality. In some ways, the history of the United States is the history of the struggle to put these words into action.

The Bill of Rights was not meant to *give* people new freedoms—it simply protects the ones people already have. For example, the First Amendment doesn't give us the right to free speech (see Chapter 3), it merely protects what we as human beings naturally have already. So it can be easy to take the Bill of Rights for granted.

But daily life without a bill of rights can be unpleasant, repressive, and even fatal. In some countries, you can be tortured, imprisoned, or killed for your religious or political beliefs. In others, you can be punished severely for relatively small offenses—adulterers are whipped in public, shoplifters can have their hands cut off. In countries where there is no freedom of the press, the government tells newspapers what to print, no matter what the real story is. When the government is all-powerful, it can tell you where to live, what jobs you can hold, how many children you can have, or even what books and music you can enjoy. Police can detain and imprison you for no reason. American immigrants from countries lacking a bill of rights perhaps know best what liberty really means.

★ ★ ★ ★ ★ ★ ★ ★ ★ ★ ★ ★ ★ ★

They are the values that define us as a people, the ideals that challenge us to perfect our union, and the liberties that generations of Americans have fought to preserve at home and abroad.
—President Barack Obama's Bill of Rights Proclamation

★ ★ ★ ★ ★ ★ ★ ★ ★ ★ ★ ★ ★ ★

Some Americans, however, don't particularly like the Bill of Rights. They think the government *should* take first place over individual rights. In fact, the Bill of Rights *has* been forgotten for many of its years.

Today, though, it has become more relevant than ever. It pops up in headlines about all the most controversial issues—school prayer, the right to choose abortion, the death penalty, gun control, pornography, censorship, the teaching of evolution, crime and the rights of criminal suspects, and much else.

Some of these topics weren't important or even around in 1791. At that time, America had fourteen states and four million people. Now it has fifty states and almost 314 million people. As times change and new situations arise, the Bill of Rights is tested over and over in courtrooms. Like Silly Putty, it's adaptable. It was intended as a living document—meant to grow and stretch with the country—rather than the last word. As new legal questions arise, they're supposed to be answered according to the Constitution and its Amendments. So 200 years later, lawyers and judges are still busy interpreting—and arguing about—these 462 very important words.

In these battles over the Bill of Rights, the ultimate authority is the highest court in the land: the *Supreme Court*. Part of the Supreme Court's role is to make the final decisions regarding Constitutional law. The Court is supposed to be the last word (though occasionally it isn't).

{ U.S. Supreme Court }

The ultimate authority in battles over the Bill of Rights.

Because of numerous Supreme Court interpretations in the last seventy-five years, the Bill of Rights has become more influential than ever before. It is said that recent justices have breathed new life into the 200-plus-year-old document. The Supreme Court has made hundreds of decisions, almost always controversial, and will make hundreds more in the future.

WHO ARE THESE GUYS?

The Supreme Court is made up of nine scholarly men—and since 1981, scholarly women. They serve on the Court for a long time—the rest of their lives, or until they choose to retire. As soon as a Supreme Court justice dies or leaves, a new one is nominated by the president and then confirmed by the Senate. Naturally, presidents appoint people who agree with their own policies. So the Court is made up of people who rarely agree with each other—because they have been picked by different presidents. Besides researching their cases, the chief justice and the eight associate justices spend much of their time arguing, trying to persuade each other to accept their points of view. When they appear in public, they wear black robes and usually appear calm.

When the loser in a state or lower federal court case appeals (protests) the verdict, the case goes to a higher-level court. Some cases keep going all the way up to the Supreme Court—the place of last resort. Its job is to review the lower-court decisions—at its discretion. It can refuse to review a decision if it wishes, and in fact takes on only 150 to 200 out of the 5,000 cases it is asked to review each year. It accepts only the very important cases—the ones that seem to raise significant constitutional issues. It decides whether the lower-court verdicts are constitutional (they fit in with the Constitution and the verdicts are upheld) or unconstitutional (they don't fit in and the verdicts should be reversed).

The cases that reach the Supreme Court are by definition not easily solved, and so its decisions always raise a ruckus. Because there are nine justices, the vote can never be a tie. The closest it can come is five to four on the *really* interesting cases—so there will always be a decision.

The Supreme Court is, quite simply, the most important judicial body in the world. It may seem remote, but its interpretations affect every American's daily life. For this reason, it's worth paying attention to who gets on the Court and what the Court has to say.

"Not Very Nice People"

In this book are some of the real-life stories behind Bill of Rights interpretations, full of drama and passion and struggle and bitter debates. The participants have been an assortment of fighters, ordinary people, and those we wouldn't necessarily see as role models.

The safeguards of liberty have frequently been forged in controversies involving not very nice people.
—Felix Frankfurter, Supreme Court Justice 1939–1962

The Bill of Rights is still being reinterpreted as it carries Americans through the twenty-first century. Many of the hardest and most persistent fighters for rights under various Amendments have been and will continue to be young people.

Why December 15 Is Amazing

One of the most passionately debated documents of all time, the Bill of Rights has been added to (see Chapter 14). But amazingly enough, it has never been formally changed.

As a cornerstone of democracy in this country, the American Bill of Rights has influenced countries worldwide. In recent years, as formerly Communist countries have established democracies, they have used our Bill of Rights as a model for safeguarding citizens against government suppression.

December 15—the date in 1791 when the Bill of Rights was ratified by enough states to become law—falls, perhaps appropriately, in the midst of our Christmas, Hanukkah, Kwanzaa, or winter solstice celebrations. President Franklin D. Roosevelt designated this as the official Bill of Rights Day at the start of World War II, when American patriotism was at an all-time high. (Later he said we were fighting the war to defend "Four Freedoms." These were a direct echo of the Bill of Rights—freedom of speech, freedom of religion, freedom from want, and freedom from fear of armed aggression.)

Franklin D. Roosevelt hailed December 15 as Bill of Rights Day.

★ ★ ★ ★ ★ ★ ★ ★ ★ ★

WHERE *IS* THE BILL OF RIGHTS?

The original Bill of Rights fits on a single sheet of 200-year-old paper (28-5/8 inches by 28-1/4 inches). It is on permanent display at the National Archives on Pennsylvania Avenue in Washington, DC, along with the Declaration of Independence and the first and last pages of the Constitution. The spidery handwriting, done with a quill pen, is seen each year by more than a million people. The air in its glass display case has been replaced with helium, to protect the paper against drying and cracking. Each night the case is lowered into a reinforced steel and concrete vault for safekeeping. You can buy an inexpensive replica at the gift shop nearby.

★ ★ ★ ★ ★ ★ ★ ★ ★ ★

The book you are holding attempts to present a balanced view of some of the issues raised by the Bill of Rights. You will probably be relieved to know that this book by no means covers everything—or it would be too heavy to lift.

But lots of famous and fascinating trials today and throughout history hinge on Bill of Rights issues. Some of these issues involve kids. As a matter of fact, a primary battleground for topics raised by the very first Amendment is the place that absorbs the biggest chunk of your time.

Where? Believe it or not: school!

CHAPTER 2

The First Amendment, Part 1—People Worshipping as They Please

★ ★ ★

*Congress shall make no law respecting
an establishment of religion, or
prohibiting the free exercise thereof.*

The year was 1986. Ten-year-old Deborah Weisman watched proudly as her older sister Merith graduated from junior high school in Providence, Rhode Island. Her only moment of discomfort was at the beginning of the ceremony, when a Baptist minister led the assembly in prayer.

"I've always felt that religion is important and has its place," Deborah put it later, "but I don't think a public school is that place."

Three years later it was Deborah's turn to graduate. In response to the Weismans' objection to the prayer, the school offered to provide a rabbi. But it wasn't because Deborah was Jewish that she had a problem with the prayer—she and her family didn't think *any* mandatory prayer had a place in public schools.

The school board, however, refused to omit it, defending it as a graduation tradition. The Weismans decided to sue on the grounds that public-school-sponsored prayer was a violation of their First Amendment rights.

What's Going on Here?

The First Amendment is an all-important and jam-packed Amendment—truly the keystone of the Bill of Rights. And it's no coincidence that religious freedom is the very first thing mentioned. It's one very hot topic.

In Deborah Weisman's case, her lawsuit took a heated path all the way to the Supreme Court. The Court shocked many by ruling in her favor in a 1992 decision called *Lee v. Weisman*. Including prayer in a graduation ceremony, the Court decided, gives any student who objects "a reasonable perception that she is being forced by the State to pray in a manner her conscience will not allow."

The Supreme Court's decision in a student's lawsuit proved controversial.

Thrilled with the controversial decision, Deborah had no regrets about her battle—despite the long wait, the hate mail she received from people who thought she was wrong, and the death threats she got from those who *really* disagreed with her.

How Religious Intolerance Can Be Fatal

Religion, because it is so intensely personal, is one of the subjects most likely to cause arguments between people and even countries. Throughout history, destructive wars have been and are *still* being fought over religious differences. In the first days of the United States, all newcomers were from Europe, with its long history of religious intolerance. Most European countries allowed one religion and forbade the practice of others; sometimes when a new king or queen took the throne the religion got switched, turning law-abiders into outlaws overnight. It was confusing, upsetting—and, when intolerance flared into aggression, often fatal.

The earliest European settlers of Virginia, for example, were from England and believed firmly in the Church of England, or Anglicanism. They showed their disapproval of others, such as Puritans, Quakers, Roman Catholics, and Baptists, by restricting their freedoms, whipping and imprisoning them, or just plain forbidding them to live in Virginia. A 1614 law imposed the death penalty on people who were convicted three times for speaking disrespectfully about the Anglican religion.

Meanwhile, in Massachusetts, those who practiced the Puritan religion believed that the Bible dictated all aspects of life, from what clothes to wear to how to have fun. Puritans tolerated no disagreement—they were even known to impose a penalty for yawning during a sermon.

In the New World, with its promise of greater freedoms, these and many other examples of intolerance seemed too much like déjà vu. Religious oppression was the reason many had fled the Old World in the first place. But several of the early American colonies were, in fact, founded by people denied the right to worship in the other colonies.

The Wall

The first goal of the 100-pound giant, James Madison (an Anglican, by the way), was to put a wall of separation between church and state. The words "separation of church and state" appear nowhere in the Constitution, it's true. But Madison's other writings make clear that this is what the First Amendment implies—a wall that would prevent the religious wars, so destructive to Europe, from crossing the ocean.

The wall is meant to work both ways: The state, or government, can't interfere with the private beliefs of people and the operation of their churches—it cannot set up a church and force you to worship there. But neither can individuals or churches impose their religious beliefs on others—you cannot force other people to believe as you do. Religious beliefs are a matter between you and your God, and the government simply has no right to interfere. Even if you are an atheist (someone who does not believe in God) or an agnostic (someone who isn't sure God exists), the government has no right to force you to believe.

The idea of a wall *sounds* simple, but problems cropped up right away. Sometimes the rules of government and the rules of a religion conflict. What happens to the wall then? Is it OK to break the law if that's what your religion requires?

The answer is sometimes yes and sometimes no. Here are some examples:

• The Amish religion teaches that modern ways, including education in public schools, should be avoided. But all states require attendance at school until a certain age. In *Wisconsin v. Yoder* (1972), a landmark case, the Supreme Court ruled that the interests of the government were not important enough to infringe upon religious freedom. Amish parents were allowed to keep their children out of public school after eighth grade.

• In 1989 the Satmar Hasidim, a small Jewish sect, created their own school district in the village of Kiryas Joel, outside of New York City. A state law permitted them to do this, allowing nearly all the village children to attend private religious schools. Twenty-two years after Yoder, the Supreme Court seemed to backtrack. In *Board of Education of Kiryas Joel v. Grumet*, it struck down the New York law as unconstitutional: states cannot intentionally create religious communities. The Hasidim were not allowed to keep their school district intact.

• Jehovah's Witnesses believe that saluting a national flag amounts to worship of an image other than a religious one. Yet most states require that kids in school salute the American flag. In 1943, the Supreme Court, reversing a controversial decision in a 1940 case involving a ten-year-old boy and an eleven-year-old girl, both Jehovah's Witnesses, ruled that compulsory flag salutes are unconstitutional.

• Some American Indian tribes make religious use of peyote, a stimulant derived from mescal cactus. But peyote is classified by the government as an illegal drug. In 1964 a California court ruled that the government's prohibition of peyote was outweighed by the First Amendment right to religious freedom. But in 1990 the Supreme Court, with different justices, upheld the dismissal of two Indians from their jobs because they had used peyote in a ceremony—ruling that when religious rights clash with government rules, the former would no longer have priority.

• The phrase "one nation, under God" in the Pledge of Allegiance bothers those who see it as an endorsement of religion. Students in over forty states are required to stand and recite it daily. Almost without exception, state and federal courts have found the Pledge constitutional, sometimes allowing students to sit and not recite it if that's their choice. Several Supreme Court justices have indicated they would find it constitutional too, and according to a poll in 2014, 66 percent of Americans agree that "under God" should remain.

• American servicemen and women used to be required to sign an oath ending "so help me God." The Army and the Navy gave permission to leave out the words without penalty. In 2014 the Air Force joined them, as it faced a court case it seemed likely to lose.

So the answers to religious questions under the First Amendment are not always obvious. And some questions are a cause for extra-loud debate.

Classrooms Are Hotter Spots Than You Think

School classrooms have been the scene of many First Amendment battles. During the 170 years following the Bill of Rights, for example, children regularly said prayers and read the Bible in public schools—schools supported by money from the government.

Then, in 1962, the parents of ten children in New York State objected. They challenged the legality of a prayer that was being said in public classrooms—they felt it amounted to what was forbidden by the First Amendment, an "establishment of religion." The case, *Engel v. Vitale*, went all the way to the Supreme Court. Much to the astonishment of many, the Court sided with the parents.

Prayer in public schools was declared unconstitutional.

"It is no part of the business of government to compose official prayers," the Court wrote. The idea of prayer was fine, but it should be left up to the individual. Voluntary prayer, such as saying grace before meals or reading the Bible in one's free time, was still legal. But organized prayer, in which all children must participate, was not.

It was a verdict that many detested. More than one hundred congressmen introduced measures that would rewrite the First Amendment to allow school prayer. Madalyn Murray, a woman who sued the Baltimore school system for requiring prayers (she and her son were atheists), became notorious as "the most hated person in America." The reaction was so fierce that President John F. Kennedy was forced to issue a calming statement. Prayer would be more meaningful, he said, when it was made part of life at home or at church rather than at school.

PRAYERS THAT HAVE LED TO COURT CASES

Almighty God, we acknowledge our dependence upon Thee, and we beg Thy blessings upon us, our parents, our teachers, and our country.
—recited by New York State schoolchildren until 1962

We thank you for the flowers so sweet,
We thank you for the food we eat,
We thank you for the birds that sing,
We thank you, God, for everything.
        —recited in DeKalb, Illinois, kindergartens until 1968

Ten verses from the Bible broadcast
each day.
        —required in Pennsylvania
           schools until 1963

The Lord's Prayer.
        —recited in Baltimore,
    Maryland, schools until 1963

One minute of silence "for
meditation and voluntary prayer."
        —allowed at the start of each   **Can Bible verses be**
    Alabama school day until 1985   **broadcast in school?**

Nondenominational prayers at public school graduation ceremonies.
        —customary until ruled unconstitutional in 1992

Student-led prayers before football games in a rural Texas district.
        —ruled unconstitutional in 2000

★ ★ ★ ★ ★ ★ ★ ★ ★ ★

Over the years, compromises have been attempted. Sometimes children are allowed to leave the room during prayer if they choose. But this has the effect of spotlighting the "oddballs," and so isn't considered fair. Some schools hold religious exercises in violation of the law and count on not receiving objections from parents, which would bring the violations to public attention. Some people think a moment of meditation, or silent thought, should be permissible; more people disagree, either because it lacks a religious emphasis, or because it seems too *close* to a religious emphasis.

In surveys, the majority of Americans (some 65 percent) do support scheduling a time for prayer in the public schools. The various Supreme Court decisions ruling it unconstitutional have therefore been particularly unpopular and difficult to accept. Critics of the decisions protest that the First Amendment merely protects atheists and agnostics—a case of the minority "tyrannizing" the majority.

But supporters argue that school prayer is too much of a step backward to what the Bill of Rights was trying to avoid: the "dark ages" of government-sponsored religion and persecution of others. They are not against the idea of prayer, but they think its place is in homes and churches, not public schools. They believe there is no way to rework the First Amendment without a loss of liberty.

★   ★   ★   ★   ★   ★   ★   ★   ★   ★

THE DIVERSITY OF SPIRITUAL BELIEFS IN AMERICA

Many of those who support school prayer would describe the United States as a "Christian Protestant" nation. But this country is much more diverse than many realize. It includes millions who do not necessarily share Protestant beliefs, including:

- Jews
- Roman Catholics

- Muslims (the third-largest religious group in the U.S.)
- Bahai (the second-largest Bahai community in the world)
- Mormons (Church of Jesus Christ of Latter Day Saints)
- Unitarians
- Hindus
- Buddhists
- Jehovah's Witnesses
- American Indian tribal religions
- people who consider themselves spiritual but do not belong to a formal religion
- agnostics and atheists, sometimes called "nones"
- antireligious people, those opposed to all religions

The Supreme Court's word on this topic may not be the last one. Since 1962, several hundred amendments have been proposed to allow prayer in public schools, though none has received enough votes to pass in Congress so far. Today many view school prayer as a way to promote values and ethical behavior in children. Others insist that the teaching of moral values does not require removing the wall between church and state. Debate over school prayer today is alive and well and, some think, more furious than ever.

SOME RESOURCES

- Guidance on Constitutionally Protected Prayer in Public Elementary and Secondary Schools (2003), U.S. Department of Education, **www2.ed.gov/policy/gen/guid/religionandschools/prayer_guidance.html**

- Religious Expression in Public Schools (2006), National Association of Secondary School Principals, **www.principals. org/portals/0/content/53841.pdf**
- Religion and Schools, American Civil Liberties Union, **www.aclu. org/religion-belief/religion-and-schools**
- Americans United for the Separation of Church and State, **www.au.org**
- Freedom from Religion Foundation, **www.ffrf.org**

★ ★ ★ ★ ★ ★ ★ ★ ★ ★

The "Monkey Trial"

One day in 1925, John Scopes, a biology teacher in Dayton, Tennessee, decided to do something daring.

A new state law made it illegal for any public school to teach anything that contradicted the Biblical story of creation, in particular

John Scopes. the biology teacher whose "monkey trial" made him famous.

the theory that human beings evolved over the course of millions of years from preexisting animals. That theory, known as the theory of evolution, had been developed by Charles Darwin in 1858. Controversial at first, it had since been accepted by scientists as an explanation of how living things change and adapt. John Scopes decided to go ahead and teach the theory of evolution in his biology class. John Scopes was arrested.

His trial—known as the "Monkey Trial" because

of Darwin's idea that humans and apes had evolved from the same ancestors—turned into one of the most sensational cases in history. Scopes was defended by Clarence Darrow, a famous and witty lawyer, and was prosecuted by the equally famous and witty William Jennings Bryan, a former candidate for president. Supporters of both sides were passionate. The impatiently awaited verdict would tell whether schools were free to teach scientific facts, or were prevented from doing so because they conflicted with certain people's religious beliefs.

The trial was expected to be brief, but it surprised everyone by lasting ten hot, sweaty days. All over the United States, it was *the* topic of conversation. If there had been television, the trial would have been broadcast on every channel.

Much to the relief of those who wish to teach Biblical theories in science classes (creationists), Scopes was found guilty and fined $100. Other states went on to ban the teaching of evolution. Most publishers of textbooks took out all mention of Darwin and his theories.

★ ★ ★ ★ ★ ★ ★ ★ ★ ★

THE "MONKEY TEACHER"

John Scopes was a balding twenty-four-year-old man who taught science and coached football in high school. He was quiet, unmarried, and well-liked—the perfect person to act as a "martyr" in trying to overturn Tennessee's new law banning the teaching of evolution. Plenty of other biology teachers were breaking the law, but Scopes volunteered to have himself arrested for it. Sue Hicks (a man named for his mother) and other young lawyers needed such a volunteer in order to get Tennessee's law tested in court so they could prove it violated the First Amendment. The group held meetings over Coca-Colas at Robinson's Drug Store on Main Street in Dayton.

As worldwide interest grew in a case that seemed to pit scientific truth against religious belief, Scopes became more of a celebrity than he had planned. After he was found guilty, he announced, "I will continue in the future as I have in the past, to oppose this law in any way I can. Any other action would be in violation of my ideal of academic freedom—that is, to teach the truth as guaranteed in our Constitution, of personal and religious freedom."

But Scopes never went back to teaching. After the trial, he received help from a number of scientists and went on to the University of Chicago, where he became a geologist.

★ ★ ★ ★ ★ ★ ★ ★ ★ ★

Then, in the 1950s, with its Sputnik program, Russia launched the world's first artificial satellites. Americans suddenly became aware that their schools' teaching of science and technology lagged far behind that of their rivals. In crash programs to catch up, textbooks became more comprehensive and again began including evolution. It was now taught in schools as established scientific fact. In 1968, the Supreme Court took on the case of *Epperson v. Arkansas* and unanimously reversed the decision in the Scopes trial. An Arkansas law

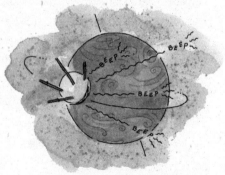

The Soviet Union's satellite program worried Americans in the 1950s.

banning evolution was declared unconstitutional because it promoted a religious belief.

Now the creationists were outraged. In Arkansas and Louisiana, they tried to get around the Supreme Court decision by requiring that biology teachers give "equal time" to evolution and creationism. Finally, in 1987, this requirement, too, was found unconstitutional by the Supreme Court. Creationism was a religious theory, not a scientific one. Requiring that creationism be taught was the same as using government "to achieve a religious purpose"—exactly what the First Amendment was supposed to prevent. The Supreme Court chimed in once more, in 2014, rejecting the appeal of an Ohio teacher who was fired for teaching creationism.

Like school prayer, the "monkey" debate is by no means a dead issue. Creationist museums have been established in at least eleven states to display evidence against evolution and for supernatural creation. The teaching of evolution is presented as Satan's greatest weapon, responsible for most of the evils in the world. One influential museum is in Petersburg, Kentucky: Creation Museum (**www.creationmuseum.org**). Founded by the Christian fundamentalist Answers in Genesis ministry, it receives some 250,000 visitors a year.

Thus, while scientists all over the world consider the case for evolution overwhelming, many people continue to believe there is no such thing. The prospect of more "monkey" trials is not unrealistic.

The Future of Religious Freedom

As important as religion was to the early Americans—so important that it rates top billing in the Bill of Rights—

the First Amendment protection for religious freedom is even more important today.

In earlier times, minorities—be they dissidents, unpopular, or merely eccentric—had the option to leave. They could move from an area where they were being persecuted and journey to the west. Today, with the country fully settled, minorities must depend on the First Amendment to protect them from the tyranny, or intolerant behavior, of the majority.

Paradoxically, the traditional American wall between church and state has caused religion to flourish here. According to studies, more people in the United States believe in God than in any other wealthy country.

Inside and outside of schools, though, religious conflicts show no sign of decreasing. Just within the span of a few weeks, cases crop up in the headlines: Should a Texas fifteen-year-old have been suspended for failing to stand for the Pledge of Allegiance? Should a Muslim player for the National Football League have been punished for kneeling in prayer after scoring a touchdown? Should a Rastafarian student have been sent home from his Louisiana high school for wearing dreadlocks as required by his religious beliefs? What about the Texas child sent home from his first day at kindergarten for wearing his long hair in a braid, according to his Navajo and Kiowa traditions? Can a city in Minnesota legally reject a proposal to build a Muslim mosque?

Recent cases that have made it to the Supreme Court have not always been clear-cut:

- What about the display of Christmas Nativity

scenes (depicting the birth of Jesus) on public property? Some who belong to religions other than Christian ones believe they indicate government support of religion. But in 1984, the Supreme Court upheld the right of Pawtucket, Rhode Island, to fund a Nativity scene in a public park, reasoning that Christmas has become a national nonreligious holiday, and that the Nativity scene was a nonreligious symbol. Again, the ruling was not the last word—argument on the subject gets renewed somewhere around the United States every December.

Christmas Nativity scenes on public property can inspire debate.

• What about displays of the Bible's Ten Commandments on public property? In 2005, the Court ruled the display in Kentucky courthouses to be unconstitutional, violating the First Amendment.

On the same day, the Court handed down the opposite verdict, that the Ten Commandments display on a Texas monument was constitutional, because the monument was both religious and nonreligious, or secular. Obviously, debate on this is ongoing.

• In 2014 (*Town of Greece v. Galloway*), the Court ruled that Greece, New York, was allowed to open its monthly board meetings with a Christian prayer. Those who think of America as a Christian nation were thrilled. Others saw it as a step backward. On the other hand, one month later, the Court agreed with a lower court ruling that a Wisconsin school district could not hold its graduation ceremonies in a Christian church.

• Also in 2014, the Court ruled in favor of Hobby Lobby, a chain of craft stores that operates "in a manner consistent with Biblical principles." Because certain kinds of birth control went against its religious principles, said the Court, the stores' medical insurance plan did not have to cover employees who used them. Justice Ruth Bader Ginsberg was one of the four who disagreed with the decision, warning of its wider implications: "The Court, I fear, has ventured into a minefield."

Despite all these and other battles, this country has succeeded in providing more religious freedom than any other country. The United States isn't likely to attempt to "cleanse" areas of certain groups, target any religious groups for extinction, or engage in religious wars that have caused so much death and destruction elsewhere.

All this and more is thanks to the First Amendment.

CHAPTER 3

*The First Amendment, Part 2—
People Speaking Freely*

★ ★ ★

Congress shall make no law . . . abridging the freedom of speech.

Mary Beth Tinker, age thirteen, was getting dressed for school one December morning in 1965 in Des Moines, Iowa. Besides her winter clothes, she wore a strip of black cloth about two inches wide around her upper left arm, over her sleeve.

Like a growing number of American students, Mary Beth passionately opposed the current American involvement in the Vietnam War. She wore the black armband as a symbolic statement of protest, a way to mourn the dead on both sides of the war. So did her brother, John, age fifteen, and their friend Christopher Eckhardt, age sixteen. Their feelings against the war ran deep, and all day long the other kids and teachers would know it.

Unfortunately, Mary Beth had barely gotten to algebra class when she was sent to the office. A few days earlier, concerned over student protest, the school board had banned armbands as a "disruptive influence." Mary Beth, John, and Chris had worn the armbands anyway. Now they were suspended from school, furious as well as frustrated at what they saw as unfairness. To them the wearing of armbands seemed like a form of free speech as protected by the First Amendment. With their parents' help, they sued the school board, and their case ended up in the Supreme Court.

It was a triumphant moment for students. In *Tinker*

v. Des Moines Independent Community School District (1969), the Supreme Court decided in the students' favor. The Court ruled that students "do not shed their constitutional rights to freedom of speech or expression at the schoolhouse gate"—meaning kids are people, too. The verdict held that the First Amendment protects the right of public school students to express their political and social views.

★ ★ ★ ★ ★ ★ ★ ★ ★ ★ ★ ★ ★ ★

Freedom to speak and write about public questions is the heart of our government.

—Hugo L. Black, Supreme Court Justice 1937–1971

★ ★ ★ ★ ★ ★ ★ ★ ★ ★ ★ ★ ★ ★

It was a controversial decision, to be sure. Mary Beth Tinker received death threats, and her house was vandalized by those who thought she was unpatriotic.

But her name is now in just about every book about constitutional law. She grew up to become a nurse at a children's hospital, and her brother John became a computer programmer. Both remained active in political protest, and in 2013 began the "Tinker Tour" to empower students to know their

Mary Beth Tinker and fellow students demonstrating freedom of speech.

rights and speak up about their political beliefs (**www. tinkertourusa.org**).

Powerful Medicine

Besides freedom of religion, the second part of the First Amendment protects the right to speak openly about what you think and feel. It's called freedom of speech—but, as demonstrated by Mary Beth Tinker, you don't have to move your mouth for it to count.

Because of the First Amendment, people in the United States have more freedom of expression than any other country in the world. We can probe the president, poke fun at government officials and protest their policies, comment on current news stories, and even criticize the First Amendment. Such privileges are crucial to democracy—they prevent the government from getting more powerful than the people.

An unconditional right to say what one pleases about public affairs is what I consider to be the minimum guarantee of the First Amendment.
—Hugo L. Black, Supreme Court Justice 1937–1971

The point of this part of the Amendment, in fact, is distrust of the government. Originally it was meant to cover only speech dealing with the political process. Over the centuries it has been used to cover plenty more opinions—about religion, current events, public personalities, ways of life. The risk of suppressing speech we don't like is that the government will also be allowed to do it. It will start telling us what opinions we *must* have. For many, this is the most crucial provision in the whole Bill of Rights.

Besides vindicating students, the Tinker decision

also enlarged the concept of free speech. Now it's considered not just words, but also symbols, actions, boycotts, sit-ins, parades, handing out leaflets, music and art, and all other kinds of expression.

The First Amendment protects this kind of music . . .

. . . as well as this kind.

48 A KIDS' GUIDE TO AMERICA'S BILL OF RIGHTS

Does this amendment extend protection to students who promote breaking the law, such as using illegal drugs? No, ruled the Supreme Court in 2007 (*Morse v. Frederick*). The case involved an Alaska student suspended for displaying a sign reading "Bong Hits 4 Jesus." In a controversial decision, the Court ruled that in this instance deterring drug use by students overruled free speech.

★ ★ ★ ★ ★ ★ ★ ★ ★ ★

SOME THINGS YOU CAN DO UNDER THE FIRST AMENDMENT

- Say things that are outrageous, or unpopular with the government or the public—some say this is exactly what the Amendment was designed to protect
- Make fun of important people
- Stand on a street and make a speech about any subject (though you may have to move if the police decide you are potentially in danger of causing accidents)
- Pass out written material about your views in public places like parks (a few states are beginning to permit this in privately owned malls as well)
- Go door-to-door and ask people to listen to your views, unless the residents have posted a sign indicating that they do not wish you to
- Walk with a group through the streets, carrying signs, speaking, or singing (you may have to get a parade license, but it cannot be denied just because officials don't like your ideas)
- Make a speech or hand out material that says other forms of government are better than American democracy
- Demonstrate against a war, even a popular one, as did those who have felt our wars in Iraq and Afghanistan were wrong

★ ★ ★ ★ ★ ★ ★ ★ ★ ★

Like freedom of religion, freedom of speech may sound matter-of-fact. Its exercise, however, stirs up powerful emotions—the words and actions of some can hurt others deeply.

> *The constitutional right of free expression is powerful medicine in a society as diverse and populous as ours.*
> —John Marshall Harlan, Supreme Court Justice 1955–1971

This part of the Bill of Rights was never intended to be a tranquilizer. Indeed, some people would put it more in the category of "bitter pill."

"Freedom for the Thought That We Hate"

It's funny—most people support free expression of ideas they agree with. Some seem to think that the Bill of Rights includes the right never to be offended.

But this Amendment protects even the opinions we loathe. Those who oppose abortion are free to display pictures of fetuses at clinics if they wish; people who admire Nazi leader Adolf Hitler have the right to say so; or someone can argue that certain races have lower IQs than others.

In a tribute to free speech, Supreme Court Justice Oliver Wendell Holmes praised "the principle of free thought—not free thought for those who agree with us but freedom for the thought that we hate."

In 1919 Holmes proposed the "clear and present

danger" test as a way to evaluate various forms of expression. If the material poses a clear and present, or imminent, danger that will bring about "substantive evils"— such as crimes or riots or other harm—then it is not protected. Otherwise it is. This test has been applied in courtrooms ever since.

Oliver Wendell Holmes urged "freedom for the thought that we hate."

The idea is that the truth—whether it supports the material or disproves it— will come out naturally, in the marketplace of ideas, and in public conversations. It should not have to be forced down people's throats by the government.

Everyone is in favor of free speech. Hardly a day passes without its being extolled, but some people's idea of it is that they are free to say what they like, but if anyone says anything back, that is an outrage.
—British Prime Minister Winston Churchill

The most recent Supreme Court decision about free speech came in 1969. In *Brandenburg v. Ohio*, the court reversed the conviction of an Ohio member of the

Ku Klux Klan, a racist organization that supports the idea that white people are superior to others. The KKK speaker had been found guilty of calling for violence against the government during remarks in which he said that blacks "should be returned to Africa, the Jew to Israel." But the Supreme Court ruled that the KKK speech, offensive as it was, had not presented "a clear and present danger," and was therefore protected. Being offended, it was implied, is the price we pay for freedom.

No other case has seriously challenged this ruling ever since.

★ ★ ★ ★ ★ ★ ★ ★ ★ ★

SOME THINGS YOU *CAN'T* DO UNDER THIS AMENDMENT

- Falsely cry "fire" in a crowded theater, or otherwise cause panic—in other words, pose a clear and present danger
- Commit a crime—murder is not considered free expression, nor is graffiti or other forms of vandalism
- Express yourself in a way likely to incite the use of force or the breaking of laws
- Make a speech or hand out material in privately owned places like restaurants or theaters unless you have permission of the manager
- Express slander or libel—deliberate lying in order to hurt a person's reputation
- Blast your radio at two in the morning—breaking the law against "disturbing the peace"
- Threaten people, as in making nasty phone calls or using blackmail to get someone to do what you want
- Say or do something obscene—offensive to community standards of decency
- Rouse an audience to the point where it gets out of control—the police can ask you to stop

- Read sexually explicit material if you're a kid—most states require that such material be placed in restricted, "adults-only" areas to which minors are denied access
- Urge the overthrow of the American government by force and violence—it will make you subject to arrest
- Make jokes about having a gun or a bomb while boarding an airplane

★ ★ ★ ★ ★ ★ ★ ★ ★ ★

Terribly distressing to many was a proposed march in 1977 by the American Nazi Party, a branch of the group that in Hitler's Germany had been responsible for the deaths of 6 million Jews. The American Nazis chose to march in Skokie, Illinois—a town where more than half of the residents were Jewish, and 7,000 of them were Holocaust survivors, or people who had escaped death from the Nazis. Thousands planned a counter-march as a protest, while the town council tried every possible legal way to stop the march.

The American Civil Liberties Union, a nonprofit citizens' group dedicated to ensuring that the Bill of Rights is preserved from generation to generation, decided to represent the Nazis in court. Thousands of ACLU members found this decision so repulsive that they resigned in protest. The Nazi Party, like the Ku Klux Klan, does not support the right of free speech for others, and many people saw no reason why these groups deserved the right themselves.

But the courts disagreed. They declared the efforts to block the march unconstitutional. One judge argued that the ability of Americans to tolerate free speech, even of hateful doctrines, was "the best protection we have against the establishment of any Nazi-type regime in this country." Another judge declared that if the First Amendment is to be meaningful in American society, those "whose ideas it quite justifiably rejects and despises" must be protected. It is *un*popular speech that needs protection—popular speech needs none.

Eventually the Nazis agreed not to march in Skokie after all. But the strife lingered. What is the point, some ask, of an Amendment that preserves principles but hurts innocent people—especially those who have been persecuted in the past? By protecting the unworthy, society is served poorly.

Others argue that hateful ideas are the very ones that should be given the light of day—brought out into the open and confronted with the truth. The cure for free speech is more free speech. Defending the right to express an unpopular opinion does not mean you agree with the opinion; you are only defending the right to say it.

Restriction of free thought and free speech is the most dangerous of all subversions. It is the one un-American act that could most easily defeat us.

—William O. Douglas, Supreme Court Justice 1939–1975

One very controversial exercise of free speech is the burning of the American flag as an expression of political protest. In two cases in 1989 and 1990, the Supreme

Court ruled that flag-burning was protected. Many war veterans and others found the thought of this, much less the sight of it, deeply disturbing. President George H. W. Bush, in calling for a whole new Amendment that would specifically protect the flag, became the first president ever to propose an addition to the Constitution that would make an exception to the First Amendment.

Ultimately, so many people disliked the idea of tampering with the First Amendment that the proposed new Amendment failed to get through Congress. Similar attempts at a flag-burning Amendment have been made ever since, and all have failed.

Still a Burning Issue

The right to free expression still causes interesting debate on all sorts of issues today.

In 1991, for example, a Supreme Court decision in the case of *Rust v. Sullivan* worried many. The court upheld a regulation imposed by President Ronald Reagan, an abortion-rights opponent; the "gag rule" banned any mention of abortion at federally assisted family-planning clinics, on the grounds that government funds were involved. One major poll showed that 64 percent of voters opposed this ruling, which did seem to violate the First Amendment by suppressing

Can the government tell librarians what to say?

speech. Most worrisome was that many institutions rely on federal money—public libraries, universities, scientific laboratories, museums, arts groups. Could the government now say what subjects can or cannot be discussed at all of these places?

In 1993, two days after his inauguration, President Bill Clinton struck down the "gag rule." In 2001, President George W. Bush reinstituted it as one of *his* first actions. In 2009, in his first week, President Barack Obama struck it down again.

Is being forced to use "politically correct" speech—language that avoids anything negative about any race, sex, religion, sexual orientation—a First Amendment violation? Or is "politically incorrect" speech just a form of bad manners, which no constitution can regulate? Many universities have imposed speech codes that ban insults and hate speech, but so far the courts have tended to rule such codes unconstitutional.

It is even unclear whether hate speech, which directly demeans or offends people based on their differences from the speaker, is protected. Also known as "fighting words," this is speech about another person's sex, race, or religion that is so insulting it is likely to provoke fights. Sometimes such speech has been protected by the court, sometimes it has not. Many feel that hate speech can't really be controlled anyway, that ignorance should be met with education, rather than elimination. Banning expressions of hate doesn't ban the hate.

Violence on TV (both in news reports and on shows), as well as online and in movies and video games, is another hot topic. Does it desensitize viewers to real-life violence? Does it give people violent ideas? Many people despise what they see as violent or tasteless material, but it's not clear that they can get it banned. With shows such as *South Park* or *Family Guy* that are not meant for kids, parents are expected to provide guidance, but can the Bill of Rights be used to protect kids whose parents are unwilling or unable to do so?

In 2011, the Supreme Court said no. It ruled that states cannot ban the sale of video games to children under eighteen because doing so would violate their First Amendment rights. Video games, even violent ones, deserve First Amendment protection. With ever-louder debate over a link between violent video games and real-life violent behavior, more court cases can be expected.

Some people find certain music offensive, and there have been numerous efforts to ban types of music as a threat to society. In the 1800s, it was ragtime music—now considered pretty harmless—that was said to cause permanent brain damage and ruin morals. Today it is more likely to be rock or rap music that is condemned. One group, the Parents' Music Resource Center, was responsible in 1990 for getting record companies to start putting "parental advisory" labels on records with what they saw to be controversial material. Musicians like Frank Zappa objected: "The PMRC's demands are the equivalent of treating dandruff by decapitation." Yet the labels stayed in use.

In 1991 two sets of parents went to court to prove their sons' suicides were related to lyrics of the rock group Judas Priest. The parents lost their case; the court ruled that the group could not have been the cause of the suicides. In 1990, the rap group 2 Live Crew was prosecuted for using obscene lyrics in their album *As Nasty As They Wanna Be*. A jury in Fort Lauderdale, Florida, however, found the group innocent. According to one juror, "You take away one freedom, and pretty soon they're all gone." After the shocking Columbine High School shootings in Littleton, Colorado, in 1999, some were quick to blame the music of Marilyn Manson, of whom the shooters were said to be fans. Manson accused the media of speculating that "artists like myself are in some way to blame," calling such scapegoating unfair.

So far, juries seem to feel that music reflects society, it doesn't create it. Banning or blaming controversial music or other material does not seem to be an ideal solution to social problems. As supporters of the First Amendment have pointed out, the sources of inspiration most often mentioned by criminals have been passages from the Bible.

As with political expression, some artistic expression *can* be worthless drivel. But who decides this? According to the First Amendment, individuals do. When the power to make these decisions is turned over to the government or self-appointed censors, it gets used in ways never intended.

Freedom of speech, it appears, does invite what some would consider abuse. But its supporters feel that *not* having freedom of speech invites greater abuse. One consequence would be mindless conformity, a climate of fear in which you let other people choose what you can and can't say and think. Depriving others of their freedom to express ideas we hate opens the door to others' depriving us of freedom to express the ideas we love.

A WORD FROM THE PRESIDENTS

Competing ideas are fundamental to freedom.
—President Ronald Reagan

Those who deny freedom to others do not deserve it for themselves.
—President Abraham Lincoln

Freedom of speech is really the freedom to think. In a way, hearing things we hate should cheer us up: it's proof that free expression is alive and well.

CHAPTER 4

The First Amendment, Part 3—What Freedom of the Press Means

★ ★ ★

*Congress shall make no law . . . abridging
the freedom . . . of the press.*

It was 1976. Lauren Boyd and Gina Gambino were the editors of their Fairfax County, Virginia, high school newspaper. They planned and wrote an article on a topic of interest to them—sexually active students who did not use birth control. The principal, however, censored their article on the grounds that the school board had a policy against teaching sex education. School officials worried that the newspaper might turn into a titillating assortment of shocks and scandals.

Very few cases of school newspaper censorship go to court, but Lauren and Gina were unusual. They decided to fight back. They sued the school board, on the grounds that their First Amendment right to freedom of the press had been violated.

A federal court, as it turned out, agreed with the girls. The judge wrote, "The state cannot constitutionally restrict anyone's First Amendment rights, including those of students, because of mere apprehension of what they might do with them." The school board's fear that the newspaper would turn into something scandalous was not a big enough reason to censor it, according to the federal court. The school board voted not to take the case further, to the Supreme Court.

It was a triumphant example of "freedom of the press" for young people.

Thanks to this part of the First Amendment, writers

across the country—in newspapers, magazines, and books, not to mention on the internet—have a freedom unmatched in the rest of the world. Walk into an American bookstore and marvel at the thousands of books from hundreds of publishers shouting the points of view of millions of people.

And we are free to read or not read what we like. Freedom of the press is an unbelievable luxury—ask anyone from a country where only government propaganda is printed or where writers can be executed for what they write. It's also of central significance to kids. While it is entirely legal for your parents to guide your reading, First Amendment problems crop up when parents try to control other kids' reading. The concept of freedom of the press frequently loses its meaning in school classrooms—those magnets for controversy.

Can Books Be Dangerous?

Cases of challenges to books—when parents don't want their child to read a book and don't want anyone else to read it either—crop up hundreds of times a year. The challenges aren't always successful in getting the books banned, or taken off the shelves, but they're disturbing to lovers of the First Amendment.

Someone once checked out every book in an Orange County, California, library that had the word "devil" in the title—even books that had nothing to do with an actual devil—and never returned them. This "stealth censorship" is supposed to guarantee that the book goes unread. It's easier to steal a book than to ban it, a formal process that tends to make challengers back down.

Can books really be dangerous?

Let children read whatever they want and then talk about it with them. If parents and kids can talk together, we won't have as much censorship because we won't have as much fear.

—Judy Blume

Censorship, or the withholding of information from being printed or distributed, has always been around. The "objectionable" topics change with the times. Literally anything can be objected to, from titles that are too difficult to pronounce, to material deemed too depressing for young people. The occult—loosely defined as having to do with devils, witches, Halloween, ghosts, magic, and so on—is one of the touchiest subjects, viewed by some as "anti-religious." Another touchy subject is any material that advocates tolerance toward gays and lesbians. Self-esteem, health and family life, religion, as well as thorny problems such as drugs, violence, racism—all of these and more are like red flags to some people.

★ ★ ★ ★ ★ ★ ★ ★ ★ ★

LOTS OF VARIETY IN CENSORSHIP

More than two centuries after the Bill of Rights, books of all types get challenged in communities around the United States. Some of the many recent challenges include:

- Captain Underpants series by Dav Pilkey—most challenged books of 2012 and 2013, for "toilet humor"
- Harry Potter series by J.K. Rowling—most challenged books between 2000 and 2009 for "occult/Satanism"
- From the Mixed-up Files of Mrs. Basil E. Frankweiler by E. L. Konigsburg—despite its Newbery Medal, challenged because it might encourage kids to run away to live in a museum
- It's Perfectly Normal by Robie Harris—a sex education book, for being explicit about "sexual activity"
- The Hunger Games trilogy by Suzanne Collins—for its "religious viewpoint"

- Twilight series by Stephenie Meyer—for being "occultic and demonic"
- *In the Night Kitchen* by Maurice Sendak—reading the book, which includes pictures of a naked baby, "could lay the foundation for future use of pornography"
- *A Light in the Attic* and other books by Shel Silverstein—"promotes disrespect, morbid"
- *Little House on the Prairie* by Laura Ingalls Wilder—offensive to American Indians
- Scary Stories to Tell in the Dark series by Alvin Schwartz—for "unacceptable violence" and "references to occult"
- *Blubber* by Judy Blume—because the main bully doesn't get punished
- *The Giver* by Lois Lowry—"unsuited to age group," among many other reasons
- *Harriet the Spy* by Louise Fitzhugh—for "teaching children to spy"
- *And Tango Makes Three* by Peter Parnell and Justin Richardson— along with others depicting gay or lesbian relationships

Censorship is the banishing of things you fear or don't like and feel you can't control any other way. Book censors try to protect kids from issues that they are exposed to in real life or other media. Thus book censorship has the effect of making

Sometimes people make a point of seeking out censored books.

books seem irrelevant to kids' lives—a bad omen for the future of literacy. Censorship also frequently has the unintended effect of making banned books seem attractive. Kids often deliberately seek these books out to see what all the fuss is about.

Censorship has no place in education.
—one of the Colorado high school students protesting the Board of Education's plan to whitewash their history curriculum in 2014

There is something in just about every book to offend *someone somewhere*. One of the functions of literature is to raise questions about the important stuff in life— and not necessarily to give the answers. To please all the different potential censors, books for children would have to become unimaginably bland drivel that would satisfy no one. Or worse—nonexistent.

So how does the First Amendment enter in?

What the Courts Say

The majority of challenges to books do not progress all the way to court, or even as far as banning and removal. The few court rulings to date usually have come down on the side of students rather than censors. They have tended to uphold students' First Amendment rights to read what they choose.

In *Board of Education v. Pico* (1982), the most important censorship case so far, the Supreme Court ruled against the Island Trees, New York, school board. The board had removed nine books from its library on the grounds that they were contrary to the community's values. Steven Pico and his fellow high school students objected. The Court declared that officials cannot remove books in order to deny students access to ideas about politics, religion, or other matters of opinion. Students' First Amendment rights are "directly and sharply implicated by the removal of books from the shelves of school libraries." Indeed, the library is an "environment especially appropriate for the recognition of First Amendment rights of students," the Court pointed out.

★ ★ ★ ★ ★ ★ ★ ★ ★ ★ ★ ★ ★ ★

All these people talk so eloquently about getting back to good old-fashioned values. . . . I say let's get back to the good old-fashioned First Amendment of the good old-fashioned Constitution of the United States.

—Kurt Vonnegut

★ ★ ★ ★ ★ ★ ★ ★ ★ ★ ★ ★ ★ ★

Censorship, according to the courts so far, seems a matter of private concern, something for individual parents to exercise with their own children. Some argue that restricting what kids read can be an easy way to avoid talk between parents and children—that *any* restrictions are not necessarily healthy. Censorship in the home may actually reflect adult disapproval of kids thinking for themselves and developing their own minds. But it's ultimately within the law.

It's when people impose their reading preferences on the rest of us that the First Amendment gets violated.

If the First Amendment means anything, it means that a state has no business telling a man, sitting alone in his own house, what books he may read.

—Thurgood Marshall, Supreme Court Justice 1967–1991

What Kids Can Print

School newspaper censorship is a much cloudier issue. Are kids in school able to print anything they want, as they would be outside of school?

After the victory of Lauren Boyd and Gina Gambino in 1976, the course of school censorship took an unfortunate turn. By 1988, the Supreme Court was giving a different kind of verdict.

Students in a Missouri high school journalism class had scheduled two articles to appear in the *Spectrum*, their newspaper—one on teen pregnancy and another on the effects of divorce on children. The principal of their school refused to allow the stories to be published on the grounds that they were unsuitable. The students went to court and ultimately to the Supreme Court.

Unfortunately for the students, the Court ruled in favor of the principal in this case, known as *Hazelwood School District v. Kuhlmeier*. Schools didn't need to tolerate student activity "that is inconsistent with its 'basic educational mission'"—even though no such censorship would be allowed outside of a school setting. The effect was to give administrators broad authority to censor school newspapers and any other school-sponsored activity. Schools were now free to "impose reasonable restrictions" on anything paid for by the school—seemingly a step backward for student freedom.

Can kids in school print anything they want in school newspapers?

It is worth noting that the makeup of the Supreme Court had changed during the 1980s—only two justices who had voted in favor of the Tinkers in 1969 were still on the court. It is also worth noting that free expression for students is still protected through unofficial channels not paid for by the school—like underground or independent newspapers, or buttons or leaflets you pay for yourself. Some states—like Arkansas, California, Colorado, Iowa, Kansas, Oregon, and Massachusetts— also have laws that give greater protection to high school students than *Hazelwood* does; check with your local office of the American Civil Liberties Union.

But as a result of *Hazelwood*, censorship cases involving school newspapers have increased, and the debate over students' right to a free press is ongoing.

Most cases of censorship involving student newspapers, however, rarely get into court—in part because students are not always aware of the First Amendment, or believe that it applies only to adults, not to them.

★ ★ ★ ★ ★ ★ ★ ★ ★ ★

HANDY RESOURCES

Places to go for more information about freedom of expression and freedom of the press:

- Student Press Law Center, **www.splc.org**
- Foundation for Individual Rights in Education, **www.thefire.org**
- American Civil Liberties Union's Project on Speech, Privacy, and Technology, **www.aclu.org/free-speech/censorship**
- American Booksellers Foundation for Free Expression, **www.abffe. org**
- American Library Association Office for Intellectual Freedom, **www.ala.org/offices/oif**
- Judy Blume's Toolkit on Censorship, **www.judyblume.com/censorship/toolkit.php**
- National Coalition Against Censorship, **www.ncac.org**
- National Council of Teachers of English Intellectual Freedom Center, **www.ncte.org/action/anti-censorship**

- People for the American Way, **www.pfaw.org**
- PEN American Center, **www.pen.org**
- *Fifty Ways to Fight Censorship and Important Facts to Know About the Censors* by Dave Marsh—see Sources and Suggestions for Further Reading, page 221.

★ ★ ★ ★ ★ ★ ★ ★ ★ ★

The First Amendment Online

It was 1995. High school senior Paul K. Kim was in the mood to play a prank. He wrote a parody of his school paper, poking fun at classmates, and put it online. He included links to sexually explicit sites.

The principal of his Bellevue, Washington, school was unamused. She responded by withdrawing the school's support of Paul's National Merit Scholarship. She also faxed letters about the incident to the seven colleges to which he had applied, jeopardizing the pursuit of his career goal as a chemist. Appalled at the severity of his punishment, Kim contacted lawyers and threatened to sue. The Bellevue School District settled out of court, allowing Kim to reapply for the scholarship and paying him $2,000 in damages. Kim went on to be accepted as a freshman at his second choice of college, Columbia University.

This case and others like it open a new can of technological worms for freedom of the press. Does the First Amendment protect users of the internet? Should obscene or potentially offensive material online be monitored or censored for children's benefit, and how can this be done without infringing on adults' rights?

The legislation about this issue has swung back and forth. In 1996 the Communications Decency Act passed by Congress alarmed many, since it proposed stringent curbs on what could be put on the internet. In 1997 the Supreme Court ruled the CDA unconstitutional (*Reno v. ACLU*). The internet was supposed to be a free speech zone, according to this ruling. A federal judge

Does freedom of the press protect the internet?

commented, "Just as the strength of the internet is chaos, so the strength of our liberty depends upon the chaos and cacophony of the unfettered speech the First Amendment protects."

But attempts to regulate the internet continued. In 1998, Congress passed the Child Online Protection Act (COPA), with the intent of restricting access to materials deemed harmful to minors. But so many people protested that the law never took effect. The Supreme Court decided on three occasions not to review COPA, and by 2009 the law was considered invalid—a victory for free speech.

On the other hand . . . in 2000 Congress passed another law, the Children's Internet Protection Act (CIPA). It requires that schools and libraries use internet filters and other measures to protect children from harmful online content as a condition for federal funding. Challenges to CIPA began immediately, but in 2003 the Supreme Court ruled it constitutional. That's where things stand—for now. Stay tuned, as our technology evolves so fast we're not always aware of its impact.

Other Hot Topics

Pornography, or sexually explicit material, raises red flags for a lot of people. Some want it censored because it offends their religious convictions and they believe it's morally wrong—for them and for everyone. Others believe it's not just offensive, but actually harmful to women, a leading cause of abuse and harassment, a violation of women's human rights on a massive scale. At the moment the laws tend to protect the pornographers, not any potential "victims" of their work.

Defenders of the First Amendment may or may not be fans of pornography, but feel that it has to be allowed to exist. Laws that ban it, they feel, will have dangerous implications, such as being enlarged to ban material that is genuinely useful to women. A ban could "protect" women at the cost of their freedom and would ally them with the religious censors of pornography—who may have an explicitly anti-feminist agenda. The argument that pornography hurts women may promote the idea of women as victims who need protection from men. Those who oppose censorship argue that time and energy could be better spent dealing directly with specific crimes against women, like rape and domestic violence.

One definite "no-no" under the First Amendment is the staging and recording of crimes. There is no freedom of the press for child pornography, because sexual acts depicting minors are illegal.

Other areas are less black and white. A magazine about marijuana, use of which is still mostly illegal, can report on its cultivation or applications, but it is not allowed to advocate its use. There can be a book called *How to Kill*, but it is not allowed to urge readers to follow the advice. Websites with instructions for making bombs are still allowed.

Making fun of important people online or in print is also allowed. In 1983 the Supreme Court ruled that the First Amendment protected a magazine that had run an ad suggesting that a famous minister had done several things too tasteless to print in this book. Ridicule that is plainly not meant as factual was therefore protected.

What about newspapers or websites that publish intimate details about famous people's lives? As rude as many people find this, it is protected—unless it sinks into libel, or lies. The actress Keira Knightley, for example, was able to sue a newspaper for falsely printing that she had an eating disorder—and she won a settlement.

One unpopular aspect of freedom of the press is that it even extends to criminals. In 1991 the Supreme Court struck down the "Son of Sam" law (named after serial killer David Berkowitz, who sent notes to the police signed "Son of Sam"). The law had made it illegal for criminals to profit by selling stories about their crimes, a restriction which most people felt was entirely justified. But the Supreme Court held that the law violated the First Amendment—even convicted criminals have rights. Some states have responded with laws requiring that profits from a criminal's book must be turned over to the victims.

One of the reasons freedom of the press is so prominent in the Bill of Rights is that the minds behind it

Can newspapers print obvious lies about celebrities?

were firmly against the government telling newspapers what to print. Instead, citizens need to know what the government is doing. If it wasn't for freedom of the press, the government could be violating all of our other rights and we wouldn't know it.

Journalists who believe that they and the public have the need to know what goes on behind closed doors run into opposition from those who believe such curiosity compromises national security.

So far the courts have tended to favor the government, saying the safety of the country takes priority over freedom of the press. This hasn't stopped many journalists, although some people worry journalists will eventually endanger security so much that the First Amendment will have to be changed to prevent them from doing so.

What about freedom of the press during times of war? Should military officials get to review or withhold news from war zones? Most people have no problem justifying censorship in this case. During the 1991 war in the Persian Gulf, all reports of it had to pass through military censors—and no public outcry ensued.

More recently, since the terrorist attacks of September 11, 2001, secrecy in government has become increasingly controversial. The attacks left Americans angry, frustrated, and traumatized. President George W. Bush declared a "War on Terrorism" as our response. Like many Bill of Rights issues in the post-9/11 world, First Amendment topics come into play once the word "war" gets used (see page 213—Chapter 15).

We will not allow this enemy to win the war by changing our way of life or restricting our freedoms.
                    —President George W. Bush, September 12, 2001

The Exhilaration of Tolerance

Freedom of the press was critical to the people who created the Bill of Rights. They came from countries where you could be killed for what you printed, especially if you criticized the government. Thomas Jefferson considered this freedom so important he said that if he was given the choice of doing without newspapers or doing without government, he'd make do without the government. Freedom of the press is freedom of information, and First Amendment defenders fear a country in which everyone thinks alike—and in accord with official government statements.

We may take freedom of the press more for granted today. But as long as tolerance is understood to mean tolerance for ideas that some will find worthless or disturbing, First Amendment battles will continue to erupt.

. . . of making many books there is no end.
                              —Ecclesiastes 12:12

CHAPTER 5

*The Second Amendment,
or People and Guns*

★ ★ ★

A well regulated Militia, being necessary to the security of a free State, the right of the people to keep and bear Arms, shall not be infringed.

Strictly speaking, the Second Amendment has little to do with kids. While boys as young as twelve and thirteen may have been expected to know how to use firearms in colonial days, most minors are not allowed to own guns today. But many young people carry guns anyway, and a growing number of them are victims of gunshots. Every day, guns kill eighty-seven Americans and injure 180 more.

With statistics like these, guns are a topic of increasing interest and concern to everyone.

And every newspaper or TV story about gun control—not to mention assassinations, accidental deaths from guns, school shootings, the National Rifle Association, murders committed with guns, and the patriot or militia movement—is a story related to the Second Amendment.

In the Eye of the Beholder

The early colonists endured a threatening lifestyle. Fierce wild animals roamed the woods, and families depended on guns for protection, and also, of course, for hunting their own food. Whenever American Indians, in response to ill treatment, became hostile, they were a genuine threat—they knew the land and its ways a lot better than the colonists did. Guns were frequently the only thing standing between the new settlers and massacre. Those who owned slaves used the fact that they had guns—and their slaves didn't—to enforce their cruel authority. There was no police force or national army—it was every family for itself. In some early states, citizens were required to be armed.

On top of everything else, the British army was right in everyone's faces, trying to impose its government on Americans. In England the rulers had disarmed the British people, making them powerless. Settlers here were nervous that the same thing could happen to them. With day-to-day life such a risky proposition, a privately owned gun literally meant freedom.

Hence the Second Amendment.

Guns were vital to early American settlers.

Unfortunately for twenty-first-century Americans, the eighteenth-century Americans were a tiny bit vague when they worded it.

"Arms" is generally interpreted as guns, but "Militia"—what does this mean? Does it mean the entire able-bodied adult population, that is, almost everyone? Then almost everyone has the right to "keep and bear arms." Or does "Militia" refer to an army of trained citizens, a military force such as the colonial-era Minutemen, which was the sole American defense against the British army? If we don't have government-sponsored militias today, is there then no need for citizens to arm themselves? If so, the only people allowed to "keep and bear arms" now would be

- the police;
- the branches of the United States military service;
- and members of the National Guard, a state system of part-time, nonprofessional organizations that are considered successors to the Colonial-era militias.

"The right of the people"—who are they? Does "people" mean all the individual people in the country? Then we all have the right to "keep and bear arms." Or does it mean the states? In this case the society as a whole would have certain people responsible for protecting it.

What about "keep" and "bear"? Why are both of these words included? Some people believe that "bear" has a strictly military meaning—only soldiers "bear" arms. Those people interpret "keep" to refer to ordinary citizens, who should therefore also be allowed to have guns.

With James Madison no longer around to explain himself, people have been arguing—sometimes in fiery terms—about these words ever since they were written.

Lawyers and legal professors usually have taken what's known as the narrower view: the right to own guns is a collective one, and each state is allowed to protect itself effectively, with a specific militia. Guns should be strictly controlled within the general population.

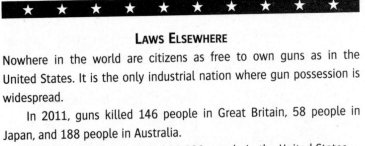

LAWS ELSEWHERE

Nowhere in the world are citizens as free to own guns as in the United States. It is the only industrial nation where gun possession is widespread.

In 2011, guns killed 146 people in Great Britain, 58 people in Japan, and 188 people in Australia.

That same year, guns killed 32,000 people in the United States.

The majority of the general population, however, feels exactly the opposite. They already have guns and don't want them taken away. They believe the Second Amendment protects the right of individual citizens to own and use guns for personal safety and political freedom.

This is possibly the most controversial Amendment in the whole Bill of Rights. Nearly everyone who reads it interprets it to suit his or her own philosophy.

The most controversial Amendment of all?

The Gun Control Debate

It is estimated that one-third of American homes contain at least one gun. There are some 300 million guns and rifles in America. People who own guns believe:

• Laws will not stop criminals from getting guns illegally.

• Gun control does not provide crime control.

• Law-abiding citizens need to fight back against criminals and should be allowed to own guns for self-protection.

• Guns are crucial to defend oneself against possible violent dictators, tyrannical groups, or terrorists, whether from outside or within the United States—an unarmed population can be easily enslaved, making guns a symbol of democracy.

People in rural areas and the Western states are more likely to take these broad views of gun ownership and therefore more likely to oppose gun control. It is estimated that some 80 percent of gun owners are white men.

★ ★ ★ ★ ★ ★ ★ ★ ★ ★

ANTI-GUN CONTROL ORGANIZATIONS

The largest is the National Rifle Association. The NRA began as a sporting organization, promoting gun safety in hunting and target shooting. When gun control became a topic of debate in Congress in the 1960s, the NRA took the side of gun owners. The right of ordinary citizens to own guns has increasingly been its focus. Now a powerful group of over five million people, it makes sure that elected officials receive great quantities of mail reflecting a "pro-gun" point of view. For more information:

- National Rifle Association, **www.nra.org**
- Gun Owners of America, **www.gunowners.org**
- Second Amendment Foundation, **www.saf.org**
- National Association for Gun Rights, **www.nationalgunrights.org**
- Citizens' Committee for the Right to Keep and Bear Arms, **www.ccrkba.org**
- Open Carry, **www.opencarry.org**
- Bearing Arms, **www.bearingarms.com**

★ ★ ★ ★ ★ ★ ★ ★ ★ ★

Those who take the narrower view—that guns should be controlled—believe:

• The Second Amendment says nothing about individuals owning guns—it only gives states the right to maintain armed militias.

The NRA promotes safety in target shooting.

- It was not meant as a "gun license" for all people.
- The right to own a gun is nowhere in the Constitution.
- Something should be done about the thousands of gunshot deaths a year in the United States. It has become a serious public health crisis that needs solutions.
- Laws could be passed to stem the flood of violence and death caused by guns.

Lately, after a wave of assassinations of prominent people and the shock of horrific school shootings, more and more citizens have been taking this narrow view.

Even if guns were once a measure of personal protection against invaders, they are meaningless against the high-tech weapons used by modern armies. People who live in urban and suburban areas are more likely to favor gun control.

★ ★ ★ ★ ★ ★ ★ ★ ★ ★

PRO-GUN CONTROL ORGANIZATIONS
- Brady Campaign to Prevent Gun Violence, **www.bradycampaign.org**
- Children's Defense Fund, **www.childrensdefense.org/programs-campaigns/protect-children-not-guns/**
- Doctors for America, **www.drsforamerica.org/learn/gun-violence-prevention**
- Everytown for Gun Safety, **www.everytown.org**
- Law Center to Prevent Gun Violence, **www.smartgunlaws.org**
- Moms Demand Action for Gun Sense in America, **www.momsdemandaction.org**
- Violence Policy Center, **www.vpc.org**

★ ★ ★ ★ ★ ★ ★ ★ ★ ★

Since the anguishing deaths of twenty first graders and six of their teachers at Sandy Hook Elementary School in Connecticut, in 2012, there have been more than 120 incidents where shots were fired on school property. Meanwhile, many children live in neighborhoods with gangs and routine gun violence. More and more citizens are speaking up in favor of gun control.

In response, those who despise the idea have raised their voices more loudly in protest.

Various Responses to the Second Amendment

All fifty states do place some limitations on the sale and manufacture of weapons, but laws vary widely and contradict each other:

- In forty-four states, it is technically legal to carry a gun as long as it is visible, with fourteen states requiring a permit.

- In response to the Sandy Hook shootings, New York State passed the NY SAFE Act, which established a database of people judged to be too mentally unstable to own a gun; by 2014 the list had grown to more than 35,000 New Yorkers.

- In Arizona, there are no age limits for firing guns; in 2014 a nine-year-old girl accidentally shot and killed her instructor at a shooting range.

- In 2014, California threw out its strict requirements for getting a concealed-handgun permit; within two months applications in some areas had multiplied by eight. This case is likely to go to the Supreme Court.

- Also in California, a 2013 law required semiautomatic pistols to stamp a unique serial number on each bullet fired from the gun.

- At least seven states allow concealed guns on college campuses.

- In the past few years it became possible to make a simple plastic gun using the latest 3D printing technology. Manufacturing such a gun is illegal in all states, according to the Undetectable Firearms Act (1988), which prohibits owning a gun that cannot be seen in a metal detector.

- Twenty-two states have a variation of the "stand-your-ground" law: a person has no duty to retreat if under attack at home or in other locations and can use any level of force. This makes it possible to shoot others and then claim self-defense. In Florida, George Zimmerman used this defense in 2012 after killing Trayvon Martin, an unarmed African American teen. In 2014, another Florida man used the same defense for shooting an unarmed African American teen playing "loud music"—but was sentenced to life in prison.

- To get guns off the streets, some states have tried gun buyback programs, in which people turn in their guns to police in exchange for money or gift cards. In 2012, one day after the Sandy Hook massacre, residents in Oakland and San Francisco turned in over 600 guns, which were then destroyed.
- In 2013 Iowa allowed legally blind people to get permits for guns.
- Also in 2013, South Dakota became the first state to allow all teachers the right to carry guns.

★ ★ ★ ★ ★ ★ ★ ★ ★ ★

How Have the Courts Helped?

The Supreme Court has been reluctant to help us figure out what all this means. In 1939, it tiptoed into the waters with *United States v. Miller*. This ruling held that the Second Amendment did not protect the right to own weapons not useful to a militia, and that the right to bear arms is a community right related to service in a militia, not an individual right.

Then, in 2008, in *District of Columbia v. Heller*, the Court ruled that the Amendment does protect the right of individuals to own guns for lawful purposes. The ruling applied only to federal properties *within* a state, such as military bases. What about the states themselves? Two years later came *McDonald v. Chicago*, which answered the question: the Amendment *did* apply to the state and local governments and allowed individuals within them to "keep and bear arms." Neither ruling ended the debate. But both sides had reason to be pleased with the rulings—the anti-gun-control side because they supported their interpretation

Interpretations of the Second Amendment vary widely.

of the Second Amendment, and the pro-gun-control side because they provided no obstacle to regulations imposed on gun ownership.

Since then, however, Court rulings have tended to keep restrictions on individual use of guns. The Court declined to hear any other NRA-backed challenges to gun control laws until 2014, when it upheld a law that forbids lying about buying a gun for another person. You can't get a third party to buy a gun for you as a way of bypassing the federal background check system. The Court seems to be supporting gun violence prevention.

Until further word from the Court, nothing in the Second Amendment restricts Congress or states from limiting the right to keep and bear guns.

WAR AND GUNS

Between 1963 and 2010 (the wars in Vietnam, Iraq, and Afghanistan), almost 65,000 American soldiers were killed in combat.

During the same period, 166,000 children and teens died of gunshot wounds in America.

Laws to help define the Second Amendment have been slow in coming. In 1981, President Ronald Reagan was shot in the chest; three other people were wounded, including the president's press secretary, James Brady, who suffered serious brain damage and eventually died. Named in his honor, the Brady Handgun Violence Prevention Act proposal was drafted in Congress.

Because of opposition from gun owners, the Brady law was defeated again and again. Finally, in 1993, it passed and became federal law, setting a waiting period of five days for handgun purchases. This delay is supposed to give police time to run background checks to make sure a gun buyer is mentally competent and has no criminal record. It also means people cannot go out in the heat of an angry moment to buy a gun.

In the fifteen years after the Brady bill's passage, 1.8

percent of firearms purchases were blocked to felons and fugitives from justice because of the required background checks.

Such laws have infuriated people with an intense distrust of the American government. They see them as taking away their right to self-defense, the government disarming them as the British did to its citizens. The bombing of the Oklahoma City federal government building in 1995, which killed 165 people, many of them children, exposed this so-called militia or patriot movement to wider scrutiny. Heavily armed and spreading around the country, the movement includes self-styled private militias, white supremacist groups, and organizations that protest various government policies—from the requirement that citizens pay taxes to its membership in the United Nations.

Many who fear government intrusion into private lives believe that the Second Amendment is the cornerstone of the Constitution, and thus gun control is the first step toward the government taking away *all* rights. The National Rifle Association, for example, has referred to federal gun-control agents as "jackbooted government thugs," an allusion to Nazi control of Germany during World War II. Worry over the government taking away individual freedoms has increased in the post-9/11 world.

KIDS AND GUNS

Every thirty minutes an American child or teen is killed or injured by a gun. They are seventeen times more likely to die from a gun than kids in twenty-five other wealthy countries *combined.* Guns are the leading cause of death among African American kids under nineteen and the second among white kids (with car accidents being the first).

★   ★   ★   ★   ★   ★   ★   ★   ★   ★

Meanwhile, movies, TV shows, and video games continue to glamorize the use of guns. Each year a growing number of children are killed with guns used by other children, or are accidentally killed by the guns in their own houses.

As a result, more and more people are using the Second Amendment to argue for stricter gun control. The Brady bill does have loopholes, which a federal law mandating universal background checks for *all* gun sales would close. Today it is estimated that 92 percent of Americans do support universal background checks, but Congress has consistently voted this measure down.

And some day, the Supreme Court may be called upon to decide a case that settles the matter once and for all.

CHAPTER 6

*The Third Amendment, or Why Soldiers
Can't Live in Your House*

★ ★ ★

No Soldier shall, in time of peace
be quartered in any house, without the
consent of the Owner, nor in time of war,
but in a manner to be prescribed by law.

You say that housing soldiers is not one of your top ten worries?

During the early days of American history, it would have been. Having the military drop in at your house was one of the biggest disasters that could happen to you. The Third Amendment assures us that those days are over.

What *Were* Soldiers Doing in Houses?

American colonists endured an amazing invasion of privacy: the British forced the new colonists to house their soldiers, or redcoats. It was their common practice to "quarter" their troops in private homes without the permission of the owners. Who *wouldn't* have found this an intolerable indignity? Americans deeply resented the presence of a standing army in their midst, not to mention the expense and inconvenience of having soldiers sitting at their tables and sleeping in their beds. Just rude. The bitterness grew into one of the biggest of the many big conflicts between the British and the Americans.

In 1768, some 4,000 redcoats invaded Boston, then a town of 16,000. Tempers really flared at this new case of quartering. With colonists having to share space with the enemy, whom they called "lobsterbacks," daily life was a matter of surviving in an occupied city.

American colonists had to share space with British soldiers.

Finally, in March 1770, fights broke out and escalated into a one-sided battle: an unarmed mob of angry Americans against a small number of redcoats with guns. Shots were fired, killing Crispus Attucks, a black American, and two teenagers—five people in all, with six more wounded. The quartering of soldiers had triggered what became famous as the Boston Massacre.

The massacre, in turn, was one of the major events leading straight to the American Revolution. When Thomas Jefferson wrote the first draft of the Declaration of Independence in 1776, the quartering of troops and the keeping of standing armies during peacetime were two of the chief complaints against the British.

Why This Chapter Is Short

In 1791, James Madison, like Jefferson, assumed a need to protect citizens from housing soldiers. But, as it turned out, the need was never to materialize again. Even by 1791, this issue was already dead—the British had long since surrendered and that era of American history was in fact over.

But Madison and others wanted to get it in writing. It was important to guarantee that (1) foreigners could never repeat this practice on American soil, and (2) the United States itself couldn't force civilians to house the military. So the Third Amendment spells out that private homes could not be set aside for soldiers' use during times of peace, and that a specific act of Congress would be needed to do so during war. The goal was to keep the military under civilian control. Just in case.

So far, civilians have stayed on top of things. The American military has never felt the urge to invade people's homes.

The Third Amendment, therefore, has been called a fossil, the "forgotten" Amendment, and kind of a mistake.

The Third Amendment in Court

The only serious case to involve this Amendment so

far is *Engblom v. Carey*. Two prison guards, Marianne Engblom and Charles Palmer, sued the governor of New York, Hugh Carey, in 1979. They and other New York prison guards had gone on strike, or stopped work until their employers met certain demands. The governor called on the National Guard to replace them. The striking prison guards had to leave their state-provided housing so that the National Guard could move in.

Two of the striking guards sued, claiming that their Third Amendment rights had been violated. Ultimately, the courts ruled against them—they "did not have the kind of property right that warrants protection under the Third Amendment." In other words, state-sponsored housing was not exactly the same thing as a privately owned house.

The Third Amendment *has* been helpful in other areas. It's been used to add support to the concept of privacy—a word found nowhere in the Constitution but increasingly the basis of various court cases involving other Amendments. If you accept the idea that "people's homes are their castles," that soldiers have no right to enter your home, then neither do intruders with other purposes.

In other countries, issues raised by the Third Amendment present much more of a nightmare. People throughout history have had to live in close quarters with soldiers, creating much tension. This Amendment *could* become relevant in the United States in the future, in ways we can't foresee.

But with military housing, American soldiers today have their own space. U.S. citizens may have complaints about their government or the military, but being forced to quarter troops isn't one of them. And it probably never will become one—as long as we have the Third Amendment.

An intrusive camera could be compared to a soldier.

CHAPTER 7

The Fourth Amendment,
or Searching and Seizing

*The right of the people to be secure
in their persons, houses, papers, and
effects, against unreasonable searches
and seizures, shall not be violated, and no
Warrants shall issue, but upon probable
cause, supported by Oath or affirmation,
and particularly describing the place
to be searched, and the persons
or things to be seized.*

Case #1: One day in March 1979 thirteen-year-old Diane Doe went to school as usual. But on that day classes at her Highland, Indiana, junior high were interrupted by the appearance of police on a raid for illegal drugs.

The students in Diane's class had to sit still while a specially trained German shepherd examined each one. After the dog showed extra interest in Diane, police ordered her to empty her purse. When the dog's sniffing continued, she was taken to the nurse's office, where she had to remove her clothes and have both her clothing and body inspected. No drugs were found. Diane was free to go. But had her rights under the Constitution been violated?

Case #2: A year later a fourteen-year-old girl known as T.L.O. was caught smoking cigarettes in her New Jersey school bathroom. In the principal's office, she denied the charge. An assistant principal searched her purse and found cigarettes—as well as marijuana, rolling papers, and lists. With this as evidence that T.L.O. was dealing drugs, authorities suspended her. Were T.L.O.'s rights violated?

A Background of Outrage

The Fourth Amendment is meant to provide protection from the government's nosiness: people and their homes cannot be searched by the police or authorities for no reason.

The background to this Amendment is outrage. The anger was aimed from the early colonists at one of the more annoying aspects of British rule. Agents of the British king, when armed with general search warrants (not based on any specific evidence), could enter and search your home at any time on any whim. They looked for things they considered illegal. Material critical of the king, for instance, or items on which the heavy British tax hadn't been paid. The agents searched everyone to find the few who were guilty. These searches with nonspecific warrants have been called the single biggest cause of the American Revolution.

Unable to protect themselves against these brutal, arbitrary intrusions, Americans reacted as soon as they could, by adding this protection to the Bill of Rights. It was meant as a slap in the face to British law.

Since then, no searches are supposed to occur unless law enforcement officers go to a judge first. They have to argue that there is probable cause that a search will uncover evidence of a crime. By obtaining a search warrant from a judge, police can still go about their business of solving crimes. But citizens are not supposed to be searched without a reason.

Uncontrolled search and seizure is one of the first and most effective weapons in the arsenal of every arbitrary government.
—Robert Jackson, Supreme Court Justice 1941–1954

In the classic Alfred Hitchcock movie *Rear Window*, the character played by Jimmy Stewart gets so carried away by the mysterious events he observes from his window that he wants to barge into a neighbor's apartment to search for evidence. A police officer reminds him sternly, "We have a Constitution." He's talking about the Fourth Amendment's provision that there can be no search without a warrant. Sometimes it's used to defend the right to privacy—the right to be left alone.

This Amendment may affect the right to be left alone.

It is, however, one of the Amendments most fought over in court.

Diane Doe's Story

According to Diane Doe (not her real last name—"Doe" and "Roe" are sometimes used to protect a person's identity), she had never used drugs in her whole life. She did, however, own a dog who happened to be in heat, and it was probably the smell of her dog that caused the police dog to get so interested in her. So besides being embarrassed and humiliated, especially by the strip search, Diane was angry. Because of the extra scrutiny, people had been spreading rumors about her, and harm had been done to her reputation.

The police had no evidence against or suspicion of any particular student that day. They had no search warrant. For all of their trouble, of the 2,780 students searched, just seventeen seniors at the high school next door were found to have marijuana or beer in their possession. But with their families' help, Diane and nine other students decided to sue the school officials, the police chief, and the trainer of the German shepherd, on the grounds that their Fourth Amendment rights had been violated.

By the time of the trial, all the families but Diane's had dropped out for various reasons. Opposition to the drug raid was not a popular move. Everyone was concerned about the presence of drugs in school, and the community largely supported the actions of the police. Even many students disagreed with Diane's decision to sue.

So, as it turned out, did the courts. The Supreme Court declined to hear her case. The lower courts ruled against Diane on everything except one aspect of her complaint: the strip search. All parts of the police raid had been justified as legitimate ways to keep the school safe and orderly, except that one. Since the authorities had no hard evidence that Diane was involved with drugs, the strip search of a thirteen-year-old was carrying "search and seizure" too far. One judge called it "an invasion of constitutional rights of some magnitude" as well as "a violation of any known principle of human decency."

As damages for the strip search, Diane received a

substantial financial settlement from the school and police. But the effect of the courts' decision was to say that students do not have full Fourth Amendment rights. Like everyone else, kids are supposed to be protected from unreasonable search by the police, but not necessarily in their roles as students. School officials aren't subject to the same standards as society as a whole—they don't need to have a warrant from a judge or information about particular students to justify a search of all students. All they need is "reasonable cause to believe" that something illegal is going on.

It is worth noting, however, that one Supreme Court justice, William Brennan, went on record to disagree with this verdict: "While school officials acting *in loco parentis* [a Latin expression meaning "in the place of the parent"] may take reasonable steps to maintain a safe and healthful education environment, their actions must nonetheless be consistent with the Fourth Amendment."

Opinions on the rights of students under this Amendment are obviously not unanimous. A search can be reasonable or unreasonable depending on who is looking at it.

New Jersey v. T.L.O.

The case of T.L.O. (her name has never been released to the public) *did* reach the Supreme Court, in 1985. Once again, the verdict about whether her rights had been violated was mixed. Students are protected by the Fourth Amendment, ruled the Court in this instance— the first time the Supreme Court had ever affirmed this. Authorities can't search everyone; they must have an "individualized suspicion" that someone in particular has broken a law.

But searches without a warrant by school officials are still permissible: "Against the child's interest in privacy must be set the substantial interest of teachers and administrators in maintaining discipline in the classroom and on school grounds." In other words, a school setting works to dilute the Fourth Amendment. Instead of "probable cause," all the school needs are "reasonable grounds"—a looser requirement than outside of school.

In T.L.O.'s case, the Supreme Court decided that the assistant principal's search of the purse was reasonable. He had been looking for evidence to support the charge of cigarette smoking. Once the search was underway, the damaging evidence justified continuing it. With this ruling, the Supreme Court overruled a lower court that had called the search *not* reasonable.

More recently, a thirteen-year-old girl named Savana Redding was strip-searched by officials at her Arizona school. No drugs were found, but she'd been identified as someone distributing prescription-strength ibuprofen. Her mother sued the school district in a case that went on to the Supreme Court. In *Safford Unified School District v. Redding* (2009), the Court ruled that Savana's search violated the Fourth Amendment.

So student rights under this Amendment continue to be of interest:

• Are lockers at school protected from warrantless searches? (The laws on this differ from state to state.)

• Are desks, cell phones, computers? What about passwords to your social media accounts?

• Are bodies—as in the use of metal detectors to prevent weapons from entering school buildings?

What about metal detectors at school?

The Seventh-Grade Football Star

And what about urine?

In 1991, James Acton was the star seventh-grade football player at his Vernonia, Oregon, public school. As part of society's "war on drugs," many schools around that time were beginning to test students' urine for the presence of illegal drugs. The school in Vernonia, concerned over increasing drug and discipline problems, particularly among its athletes, required all students to take the test before being allowed to join the football team.

For males, the test involved standing at a urinal while a male teacher stood behind them. James Acton refused to do it. Such testing, he claimed, amounted to an invasion of his privacy and a Fourth Amendment "unreasonable search"—of his urine in this case. It was intrusive, embarrassing, and unconstitutional. No one suspected that he was using drugs. But because he wouldn't take the test, he was not allowed on the team.

With the help of his parents and lawyers, James's case went all the way to the Supreme Court. In 1995, in *Vernonia School District v. Acton*, the Court ruled against him: public schools *can* require random drug testing of student athletes whether or not they are suspected of drug use. The decision was controversial, particularly because it seems to open the door to even broader drug testing.

"My word should be good enough," said James, disappointed with the ruling. The Court, however, seemed to disagree, indicating that privacy rights were not the issue here. It was more important to stress that "deterring drug use by our nation's schoolchildren" is a significant weapon in the war against drugs, and drug use in schools should therefore not be tolerated. One justice pooh-poohed James's privacy concerns by saying that "school sports are not for the bashful."

A few years later, a student named Lindsay Earls got called out of choir practice to take a urine test. She sued her Tecumseh, Oklahoma, school district for requiring students to have this test before going out for any extracurricular activity. The twists and turns in this case show the thorniness of the issue: the district court sided with the school, while the court of appeals reversed that decision. The Supreme Court finally weighed in, with *Board of Education v. Earls* (2002), ruling that mandatory drug testing in public schools was constitutional.

The Court called the public school system the "guardian and tutor of children entrusted to its care." But adults are having their privacy invaded in this way as well—an increasingly common method of attempting to insure a drug-free workplace is to test employees' urine for the presence of illegal drugs. So far, workplace tests have been upheld by the courts—especially in jobs related to public safety—more often than not.

Vomit, National Security, and Other Search-and-Seizure Issues

Evidence obtained through illegal (warrantless) search and seizure is not supposed to be introduced in courtrooms, according to this Amendment. This point gets mentioned in courts daily.

★ ★ ★ ★ ★ ★ ★ ★ ★ ★

SEARCHES THAT JAMES MADISON PROBABLY DID NOT FORESEE

- emails
- computer files
- cell phone conversations
- blood tests for alcohol consumption or the presence of the virus that causes AIDS
- electronic eavesdropping with wiretaps that secretly record conversations
- camera surveillance by helicopter or drone
- trash cans
- lists of movies rented from Netflix
- records of books checked out of the library
- credit card transactions
- medical history records from insurance companies
- financial records from the Internal Revenue Service
- patterns of heat detected inside a house with a thermal imaging device (for those suspected of growing marijuana)
- GPS data from your car

★ ★ ★ ★ ★ ★ ★ ★ ★ ★

Searching people's trash is a new twist on the Fourth Amendment.

In some cases, believe it or not, warrantless searches provoke no argument. Especially after the attacks on 9/11, everyone is concerned over security at airports and on airplanes—no one wants to be hijacked or to fly on a plane with guns or bombs. The searches we all endure at airports—walking through metal detectors, putting our shoes and luggage through X-ray machines, and, if asked, letting ourselves be searched—are generally accepted. Most people agree that the chance of catching someone who threatens our safety aboard an airplane far outweighs the inconvenience of having everyone searched in a fair, efficient manner.

Airport searches provoke little argument.

If there is probable cause to believe drivers are drunk, they can be stopped at any time by police and asked to have their blood, saliva, or breath tested for the presence of alcohol—a particularly personal type of search. Most people, believing that drunk drivers belong off the road, have little problem with this. But what about random checkpoints—the roadblocks that are set up by police to test *every* driver?

In 1990, the Supreme Court upheld this practice, even though it seems to violate the rights of drivers who have shown no behavior indicating drunkenness. The stop is too brief to be intrusive, ruled the court, and when every car is stopped, no one driver is being discriminated against. The intrusion is slight compared to the legitimate concern of preventing drunk driving. The Supreme Court's decision has been controversial—several states have outlawed such checkpoints—and may not be the final word.

What about the contents of computers and cell phones? The Supreme Court chimed in on this issue in a 2014 landmark case. Eighteen-year-old David Leon Riley had been stopped for a routine traffic violation. The officer searched the car, found two guns, and started scrolling through Riley's smartphone. The officer used the contents of the phone to link Riley to gang activity, specifically a shooting weeks before. The officer lacked a warrant, and the Court did not approve. In *Riley v. California*, it ruled that a warrant is required to search a cell phone.

In an echo of the ruling, the Apple company went on to make its latest iPhone "police-proof"—with security features that prevent access to a locked phone.

The ruling also encouraged Congress to close loopholes in 1986's Electronic Communications Privacy Act, in an effort to give emails the same protection as cell phones.

So what about the contents of your stomach? In 1952 the Supreme Court did protect vomit. It reversed the conviction of a man who had been tried on the evidence produced when police took him to the hospital and had his stomach pumped—two tablets of illegal morphine. The search was not only offensive to the squeamish, the Court decided, it was illegal.

An Erosion of Rights?

In recent Fourth Amendment cases, the Supreme Court relies on an "expectation of privacy" concept. The Amendment applies most strongly in places where there is an expectation of privacy, like your home. In other words, the Amendment reinforces the idea that "every man's/woman's house is his/her castle." But continuing quarrels are certain in an age when more and more information about us is found *outside* the home. Public records now provide a lot of information that the Bill of Rights writers would probably have considered private. The Supreme Court hasn't necessarily protected that information:

• In 1979 it ruled that a robbery suspect could not keep private the phone numbers he called.

• In 1976 it ruled that bank records were information that had been revealed to a third party (the bank) and so were not protected.

• In 1988 it ruled that a person should have no right to expect privacy in regard to his trash—the items in a person's garbage could be used as evidence against him.

With the Supreme Court's reluctance to protect public information from searches, state laws have been used more and more as protection.

The point is that innocent people are supposed to be protected against unreasonable searches.

SEARCH AND SEIZURE ELSEWHERE

Police in South Africa, France, Japan, and other countries have much broader powers to search and seize without a warrant. In the United

Kingdom, the government has installed so many surveillance cameras that it's estimated that the average Londoner shows up on film three hundred times a day.

In 1994, out of fear of crime, a decree was issued in Russia that gave police the power to search homes, offices, and cars without any evidence that a crime had been committed. They can also detain just about anyone they want for 30 days without charges. Police are allowed to go through the bank accounts of people suspected of crimes, and even to investigate anyone who has lived with a suspected criminal for more than five years. This nearly absolute power of the often corrupt police has been a recurring theme throughout Russia's history. During its most repressive times it has been the first step in programs that led to the deaths of millions.

★ ★ ★ ★ ★ ★ ★ ★ ★ ★

"National security" is the basis for some searches. Following the 1995 bombing of the Oklahoma City federal building, laws were proposed that would broaden the government's authority to fight domestic terrorism. For the sake of public safety, some lawmakers wanted to target unregulated civilian militia organizations and other political extremists. Spying on suspicious groups, use of wiretaps, searches without a warrant, seizing weapons without a warrant—such tactics in the service of national security sounded to many Americans like a sacrifice of Fourth Amendment rights that could lead to uncontrolled official spying.

And indeed, a month after the terrorist attack of 2001, in a climate of fear of foreign terrorism, Congress passed the USA Patriot Act. Working against the Fourth Amendment but deemed necessary at the time, this act greatly expanded the government's power to conduct surveillance. The National Security Agency (NSA) went into high gear, defining *terrorist* very broadly, conducting limitless and warrantless searches of emails, texts, phone calls.

This surge in spying alarmed many. Especially a man named Edward J. Snowden, who actually worked for the NSA as a senior analyst. Believing that the First and Fourth Amendments were being sacrificed, he decided to blow the whistle. In 2013 he began leaking secret documents that revealed the extent of government spying—on ordinary Americans, as well as people in countries around the world and their leaders. Many were horrified and agreed with Snowden that this was unconstitutional.

The Constitution is the highest law of the land, which cannot be violated in secret in the name of a false security.

—Edward J. Snowden, 2014

Some saw him as a patriotic hero, but enough saw him as a traitor that he had to leave the country. Dealing with death threats and knowing that he would face criminal charges that would lead to life in prison, he applied for political asylum to almost two dozen countries, and eventually ended up in Russia.

RESOURCES:

- American Civil Liberties Union, Students' Rights, **www.aclu.org/technology-and-liberty/students**
- Privacy SOS: Sunlight on Surveillance, **www.privacysos.org**
- Electronic Frontier Foundation, **www.eff.org**
- Electronic Privacy Information Center, **www.epic.org**
- American Civil Liberties Union, **www.aclu.org/national-security/secrecy**
- National Security Agency, **www.nsa.gov**

Snowden's actions inspired furious and continuing debate about the balance between privacy and national security. Court cases so far on the constitutionality of the NSA's practices have been divided. But in 2014 the House of Representatives voted to start putting limits on NSA searches.

Under the Fourth Amendment, privacy and justice for all will always be a cause for unusual interest.

CHAPTER 8

The Fifth Amendment, or Criminal Justice

★ ★ ★

No person shall be held to answer for a capital, or otherwise infamous crime, unless on a presentment or indictment of a Grand Jury, except in cases arising in the land or naval forces, or in the Militia, when in actual service in time of War or public danger; nor shall any person be subject for the same offence to be twice put in jeopardy of life or limb; nor shall be compelled in any criminal case to be a witness against himself, nor be deprived of life, liberty, or property, without due process of law; nor shall private property be taken for public use, without just compensation.

With the next four Amendments, the focus switches to topics of enduring fascination: crime and courtrooms.

Most of the criminal issues covered by the Bill of Rights don't usually affect kids directly. But it's useful and interesting stuff to know. Through televised real trials and thousands of made-up plots, kids are more aware of courtroom maneuvers than ever before.

For example, you've seen this trial scene in at least a dozen TV shows: someone on the witness stand, in answer to a question, says, "I refuse to answer on the grounds it may incriminate me. I take the Fifth."

The Fifth Amendment, that is. The wording is so familiar that this is the Amendment in the Bill of Rights that most people know by number. Taking the Fifth. What *is* it?

"Infamous" Crimes

Criminal justice was obviously much on the minds of the early Americans. Altogether, the Constitution includes almost two dozen separate rules about how criminal trials should be conducted.

The people who created the Bill of Rights had just freed themselves from a heavy-handed, oppressive government. They were most anxious to stay that way. It was a time when innocent people were often accused of crimes. Being thrown into dungeons with no hope of escape, being tortured into confessions of things they hadn't even done, being imprisoned with no charges and no witnesses, having property seized for no reason—these were their worst nightmares.

The Fifth Amendment, therefore, contains a whole lot of rules having to do with the protection of an individual accused of capital or "infamous" crimes, that is, serious crimes that can be punished by death or prison. For example, it provides for a grand jury—a panel of twelve to twenty-three citizens, that holds hearings to determine whether there is enough evidence to justify a trial. They determine whether a crime has even taken place, *before* a regular jury is called upon to decide guilt or innocence.

It's all about protection of the innocent.

What Taking the Fifth Really Means

The First Amendment protects your right to speak freely—*this* one protects your right to stay mute.

When accused of a crime, you have the right to remain silent if you feel that something you might say could be used to convict you. No one can force you to incriminate, or act as a witness against, yourself.

This provision is based on the idea that, according to American law, you are innocent until proven guilty. This is not necessarily the case in some other countries, where the criminal code holds just the opposite— that you are guilty until proven innocent. In the United States, if you are charged with a crime, *you* are not required to prove your innocence. Instead, it is the *government's* responsibility to prove you are guilty—beyond a reasonable doubt, of course. It has to do so without your help. Any confession from you must be purely voluntary.

Guilty or innocent:
American law decides.

As much protection as the right to remain silent gives us, it is not always popular. Critics assume that it protects the guilty. If you won't talk freely, wouldn't it be because you have something to hide?

The answer is that some believe that the price for this right is an occasional case where the guilty *are* set free. But the benefit is held to be greater: the innocent will not get punished.

What Kind of Game Is Double Jeopardy?

Another right protected by the Fifth Amendment is

that you do not have to stand trial for the same charges more than once. If you did, it would be called "double jeopardy."

Why would this be so unpleasant? Because without protection against double jeopardy, the government could try you over and over again until it discovered a way to change an "innocent" verdict to a "guilty" one. If the government wanted to persecute you for some reason, it could force you to endure trial after trial—a form of psychological torture. Only if legal errors are committed can a person in the United States be tried twice for the same crime.

★ ★ ★ ★ ★ ★ ★ ★ ★ ★ ★ ★ ★ ★

The State with all its resources and power should not be allowed to make repeated attempts to convict an individual.
—Hugo L. Black, Supreme Court Justice 1937–1971

★ ★ ★ ★ ★ ★ ★ ★ ★ ★ ★ ★ ★ ★

So, for example, when Los Angeles police in the Rodney King beating case were found innocent in 1992, resulting in riots, the police could not be retried on the same charges. Federal authorities had to bring new charges in order to stage the second trial, which resulted in a guilty verdict. In 1996 and 1997, the two murder trials of O. J. Simpson were not the same. The first was a criminal trial, in which a jury found him innocent. The second was a civil trial, requiring a lesser burden of proof, brought by the families of the victims to obtain monetary damages (for more on civil trials, see Chapter 10).

Being Made Aware of Your Rights

Even with the Bill of Rights in place, it used to be common for police to use physical and psychological pressure to force people to confess. The police were under no obligation whatsoever to inform people of their rights under the law.

All that was before the most famous Fifth Amendment case ever to come before the Supreme Court: *Miranda v. Arizona*, in 1966.

WHO WAS MIRANDA AND WHAT DID SHE DO?

In 1963, police arrested Ernesto Miranda (a man) in his Phoenix, Arizona, home. At the police station, an eighteen-year-old girl identified the twenty-three-year-old truck driver as the man who had kidnapped and raped her. Miranda confessed after two hours of questioning. His confession was used against him at his trial. He was found guilty and sentenced to two twenty-to-thirty-year terms of imprisonment.

Ernesto Miranda confessed after hours of police questioning.

Miranda's lawyer, however, appealed the verdict on the ground that Miranda had been pressured to incriminate himself. He had not been told that, according to the Bill of Rights, he had the right to remain silent, or that anything he said could be used against him in court, or that he had the right to have a lawyer present. Without knowing these things, he had been forced to act as a "witness against himself." Therefore Miranda's confession could not be used as evidence.

The Supreme Court eventually agreed and reversed his conviction. Ernesto Miranda got to start over and have a new trial. Using evidence other than his confession, he was convicted and sent to prison again. After being paroled, he worked as a deliveryman until 1976, when, at age thirty-four, he was stabbed to death in a bar fight. The suspect in his murder was read his Miranda rights at the time of the arrest.

This was a blockbuster case that made powerful changes in the way society functions. The Supreme Court, ruling that people had to be told of their right to remain silent and consult a lawyer, wanted to give explicit protection to those most in need of it—"the poor, the ignorant, and the unwary," as the justices put it. Ever since then, people accused of a crime are supposed to get "Mirandized"—read their Fifth and Sixth Amendment rights.

The decision was fantastically controversial. Critics say that it makes it practically impossible to get anyone to confess to a crime. Some even feel lawyers are now actually getting in the way of police. It's especially awkward for police to be educating possible criminals about their rights when it's the job of the police to catch these people. Some officers ignore *Miranda* or find ways to thwart its intent.

Other police officers and lawyers praise *Miranda* for making police work more professional and sophisticated. Since people can no longer be intimidated into

THE FIFTH AMENDMENT 129

confessing, the quality of detective work has improved.
Evidence can be discovered that makes a confession
unnecessary. The change seems to have sped up the
progress of technology such as DNA matching and
fiber analysis.

Some who violently opposed *Miranda* at first now
ardently support it—and even criticize recent Supreme
Court decisions that have allowed for various exceptions
to *Miranda*. Finally, almost all surveys show that
the percentage of suspects who confess hasn't really
changed. Most of those arrested waive, or choose not to
use, their *Miranda* rights—in other words, they do talk
to the police, usually out of a powerful urge to appear
cooperative.

★ ★ ★ ★ ★ ★ ★ ★ ★ ★

THE MIRANDA WARNING

When arresting a person, a police officer must formally recite the
following four warnings and two questions:

1. You have the right to remain silent.
2. Anything you say can be held against you in a court of law.
3. You have the right to talk to a lawyer and to have the lawyer
   present before and during questioning.
4. If you cannot afford to hire a lawyer, one will be appointed to
   represent you before and during questioning if you wish one.
5. Do you understand each of these rights I have explained to you?
6. Having these rights in mind, do you wish to talk or not talk to us
   now?

★ ★ ★ ★ ★ ★ ★ ★ ★ ★

Miranda has special relevance to young people accused of crimes. Being arrested is one of the most stressful experiences you can endure. It can be particularly intimidating to kids. Knowing that you do not have to be alone and that you have the right to get help from a lawyer or another adult you trust can make dealing with it easier.

The Innocent versus the Guilty

Does it seem weird that the Bill of Rights has so much to say about the rights of criminals? What about the victims? Does our concern with possible criminal behavior on the part of the police benefit the real criminals?

The Bill of Rights, however, was never intended to protect the guilty. It was meant to protect innocent people from being accused unjustly. Under a too-powerful government, lack of this protection constitutes abuse.

Throughout history and up into our post-9/11 era, crime-fighting proposals tend to expand government power at the expense of the rights of the innocent. This is where the Bill of Rights is supposed to come alive. Those charged with crimes are human beings, and they need protection.

Paradoxically, this serves the interest of the broadest segment of society. It is in *everyone's* best interest that a person convicted of a crime is the person who really committed it.

Thanks to the Fifth Amendment, the government is supposed to "play fair." It can't grab you, stick you in prison, and hope that you will say something they can use to find you guilty of a crime. It can't refuse to let you call a lawyer or another supportive person until you sign a confession. It can't threaten terrible consequences unless you confess, or deceive you with false legal advice, or keep you off balance with other deceptive means.

Instead, with the Bill of Rights, the government guarantees that you will have "due process of law." This is supposed to give you protection against arbitrary police behavior. You're not supposed to be framed for crimes you didn't commit just because people don't like your age, race, religion, looks, or something else about you.

The Fifth Amendment doesn't always work perfectly. Instances of racial profiling are being spotlighted— police stopping people because of their race. See Chapter 15 for more times when it hasn't worked well.

But when compared to other systems around the world, the American approach to criminal justice strikes many people as the best around. In many parts of the world, people are tortured until they confess to crimes. In other countries, many are punished on the assumption that a few of them are guilty.

In the United States, laws are guided by the belief that it is better for some guilty individuals to go free than for one innocent person to be wrongfully found guilty. Madison's influence here was a legal scholar who had written, "It is better that ten guilty persons escape than one innocent suffer."

This price may seem high, but the benefit is seen as even greater—freedom for the innocent.

CHAPTER 9

*The Sixth Amendment,
or More Criminal Justice*

★ ★ ★

*In all criminal prosecutions, the
accused shall enjoy the right to a speedy
and public trial, by an impartial jury of
the State and district wherein the crime
shall have been committed, which district
shall have been previously ascertained
by law, and to be informed of the nature
and cause of the accusation; to be
confronted with the witnesses against him;
to have compulsory process for obtaining
witnesses in his favor, and to have the
Assistance of Counsel for his defence.*

The year was 1964. Gerald Gault was fifteen when he was taken into custody by an Arizona sheriff. His parents weren't told that he had been arrested. He wasn't told of any of his rights under the Fifth and Sixth Amendments. In particular, he was not informed of the charges against him.

It turned out that a neighbor had complained that he had made a "lewd or indecent" phone call. The punishment for an adult making an obscene phone call would have been a $5 to $50 fine or imprisonment for up to two months. The judge decided that Gerald, who was on probation for an earlier petty theft, was a "delinquent child." For making a prank call, Gerald was sentenced to six *years* at an institution for juvenile offenders.

Gerald's parents appealed the verdict on the grounds that his constitutional rights had been violated.

How does the Sixth Amendment fit in?

"A Speedy and Public Trial"

The Sixth Amendment gangs up a list of more of the rights people have when they're accused of a crime. These are trial issues that fill in the background for things you've seen on TV.

This Amendment guarantees, for example, the right to a fast, public, and fair trial in criminal cases. It was a response to the British practice of lengthy interrogations and secret inquisitions—a burden that weighed heavily on the colonists. People could be arrested and held for years without a trial, punishing the innocent as well as the guilty. Likewise, secret trials created a climate of fear. A government can strike back at opponents by not allowing people to witness accusations and punishments that may be unjustified.

As a result, trials in the United States today are public, giving a measure of protection for the accused. Though most people involved would question how "speedy" the process is—trials have been known to take months, even years—this amendment puts the burden on the government. It is supposed to act as quickly as the circumstances permit.

American trials are supposed to be speedy.

"An Impartial Jury"

The concept of trial by jury was such a hot topic that this is the only Bill of Rights item also protected in the Constitution. It was worth mentioning not once but several times. This is also the Sixth Amendment right that was most widely recognized by the states—eleven of the first fourteen states mentioned trial by jury in their constitutions.

★ ★ ★ ★ ★ ★ ★ ★ ★ ★ ★ ★ ★ ★

Why do we love this trial by jury? It prevents the hand of oppression from cutting you off.

—Revolutionary War hero Patrick Henry

★ ★ ★ ★ ★ ★ ★ ★ ★ ★ ★ ★ ★ ★

Juries are usually composed of twelve people who represent your "peers," a cross-section of your local community. They are supposed to be impartial, meaning they haven't taken sides before the trial even begins. Before the Bill of Rights, juries were just the opposite. They were made up of men who knew the people involved and who were expected to find the accused guilty. It was the height of unfairness.

Today the jury process begins with a random selection of names from lists, such as those of registered voters or people with driver's licenses. The weeding out of jurors with obvious prejudices or other problems can be a simple or complex matter, depending on the trial. In high-profile cases, prospective jurors have to fill out a questionnaire with lots and lots of questions.

A balanced jury is supposed to be important to a fair trial, but American juries have not necessarily been

balanced. Numerous court battles have been waged to
insure that African Americans and Mexican Americans
are called for jury duty. Women were completely
excluded from juries until 1920, when they won the
right to vote. But as recently as the 1960s, many states
held that women could volunteer for juries, but weren't
required to do so. Today the only people automatically
excluded from juries are non-English-speakers, citizens
of a country other than the United States, sufferers of a
mental disorder, and those convicted of serious crimes.

Sometimes freedom of the press (under the First
Amendment) can clash with a defendant's right to a
fair trial. Extensive media coverage of a crime can
make it difficult to find jurors who are still impartial. If
necessary, a lawyer can request a "change of venue," to
move the trial to an area where pretrial publicity has not
been as great. This came up in 2014, when lawyers for
Boston Marathon bombing suspect Dzhokhar Tsarnaev
asked a judge for a venue change, arguing that a fair
trial would be impossible in Boston, the scene of the
horrific crime. A federal judge denied the request.

Gerald Gault and Being "Informed of the Accusation"

You would think that a person accused of a crime would
know what the crime was. Not necessarily.

In the past—and even today in some places around
the world—people have been and are jailed for years
with no specific charges. If you don't know the charges
against you, you can't defend yourself against them.
There is no way you can prove your innocence and be
freed.

Again, this was a cruelty that the Bill of Rights

sought to prevent. In countries without such protection, dictators can arrest and imprison people for years without having to give a reason.

Not knowing the charges against him at first was one of Gerald Gault's problems in 1964. And with the landmark case of *In re Gault* (1967), the Supreme Court agreed. By ruling in his favor, the Court noted that because of the serious consequences of criminal hearings, even juveniles should be guaranteed the protection of the Constitution.

Gerald Gault was released from reform school. (He went on to serve in the military and become a teacher.)

"Confronting the Witnesses"

The right to confront witnesses was another provision meant to thwart a basic unfairness. In order for a case to come to trial, there must be witnesses, evidence, or both. It isn't enough to tell a judge, "Everybody knows these people are drug dealers." Someone—either a citizen or police officer—has to confront the accused face-to-face at a trial.

When accusers can remain anonymous, people who don't like you can get you in trouble. You have to have the power, through your lawyer, to ask questions of accusers and to challenge their version of events.

This is especially relevant to kids in cases of child abuse. For young children, it can be traumatic to relive their experiences while those who may have harmed them are sitting in the same courtroom. And yet *not* being able to confront the children deprives the alleged abusers of their rights under the Sixth Amendment.

The Supreme Court has so far ruled in favor of

children. In *Maryland v. Craig* (1990), it decided that certain child abuse victims may give their testimony on closed-circuit TV and do not have to come face-to-face with those they accuse. The government's interest, wrote one justice, "in the physical and psychological well-being of child abuse victims may be sufficiently important to outweigh, at least in some cases, a defendant's right to face his or her accusers in court."

"Obtaining Witnesses"

If you are accused of a crime, you need all the help you can get. You need to be able to bring in information from those who might prove your innocence—"witnesses in your favor." But what if those people are too busy or scared, don't like you, or just plain don't want to come to court? Then you can make them come. The Sixth Amendment provides for a "compulsory process" known as a subpoena. A subpoena is an offer people can't refuse—a legal order to appear in court and testify.

At first, only prosecuting lawyers had the right to subpoena witnesses. But ever since the Supreme Court ruling in *Washington v. Texas* (1967), all states must allow the accused person to subpoena witnesses as well. Witnesses can be:

- bystanders who happen to know something relevant
- friends who can help clear you
- experts in specialized areas who can provide information in your favor (expert witnesses must be paid for by you, though; often only wealthy defendants can use them)

Blockbuster Cases Involving the "Assistance of Counsel"

As familiar as some of the rules covered by the Sixth Amendment may sound, they're not always crystal clear. Several landmark Supreme Court cases have helped to spell things out.

"Counsel," for example, means a lawyer, someone trained in the law who knows how to defend people in court. Thanks to the Sixth Amendment, you don't have to master the intricacies of law and defend yourself.

The importance of a lawyer was affirmed by *Escobedo v. Illinois* (1964). Danny Escobedo had been arrested for the murder of his brother-in-law in Illinois. During police questioning, he kept asking to see his lawyer. Meanwhile his lawyer was at the police station, repeatedly asking to see Escobedo. All requests were refused. At his trial, statements Escobedo had made during questioning were used against him. He was found guilty and sentenced to life imprisonment. He appealed on the grounds that his Sixth Amendment rights had been violated.

The Supreme Court agreed with him. They overturned his conviction, and the murder charges were dropped. Incriminating statements could not be used in court if the suspect had asked for and was refused a lawyer. One justice wrote, "No system worth preserving should have to *fear* that if an accused is permitted to consult with a lawyer, he will become aware of and exercise these rights."

As for Escobedo—he went on to be jailed for other crimes.

★ ★ ★ ★ ★ ★ ★ ★ ★ ★ ★

THE SCOTTSBORO CASES

Two of the first famous Sixth Amendment cases involved the same nine poor, uneducated African Americans, ranging in age from twelve to twenty. In 1931 they were pulled off a train near Scottsboro, Alabama, and accused of raping two white girls on the train. The defendants couldn't afford to pay a lawyer, and none of the lawyers in Scottsboro would agree to represent them for free. All were found guilty and sentenced to death. Newspapers around the country began referring to the trial as a "legal lynching," or a state-sanctioned attempt at hanging by an unruly mob. When the case, known as *Powell v. Alabama* (1932), reached the Supreme Court, it ruled in the defendants' favor: the state had violated their right to counsel under the Sixth Amendment.

The nine men from Scottsboro. Alabama.

The defendants, however, were not set free. They were tried twice more, and in 1935 their case came before the Supreme Court again. In *Norris v. Alabama*, the Supreme Court ruled that their Sixth Amendment rights had been violated in another way. This time it was because their case had been heard by an all-white jury; in Alabama in the 1930s, African Americans were never called for jury duty.

Despite the victory, the last of the defendants was not released until 1950.

★　★　★　★　★　★　★　★　★　★

Another blockbuster case starred Clarence Earl Gideon, who had left school at age fourteen and become a gambler and petty thief. In 1961, he was arrested in Panama City, Florida, on charges of breaking and entering a pool hall with the intent to steal money.

When he was asked at his trial if he was ready to begin, Gideon said, "I request this court to appoint counsel to represent me in this trial."

The judge refused on the grounds that Florida law supplied lawyers only in capital, or serious, cases. Gideon, who had no money for a lawyer of his own, was convicted and sent to jail for five years. He began studying law in the prison library, eventually writing a letter on prison stationery to the Supreme Court to ask for review of his case.

To many people's surprise, the Supreme Court, in *Gideon v. Wainwright* (1963), ruled in his favor: people do not just have the right to a lawyer—the courts are required to provide one. This landmark case proved that one individual can make a great difference. It has also served, ever since, to provide poor defendants with a lawyer for free in state felony cases. When governments are spending large amounts of money to prosecute defendants, and defendants with money naturally hire the best lawyers they can afford, poor defendants are at a disadvantage in defending themselves adequately.

Gideon won himself the right to a new trial. This time a lawyer was able to present the facts of the case in a different light. Gideon had worked part-time at the pool hall and had a key, and his pockets were full of change because he was a frequent card player. This jury found Gideon innocent.

Clarence Earl Gideon wrote to the Supreme Court from his prison cell. He died of tuberculosis, still poor, in 1972.

GIDEON'S LEGACY

Any person haled [forced] into court who is too poor to hire a lawyer cannot be assured of a fair trial unless counsel is provided for him.
—Hugo L. Black, Supreme Court Justice 1937–1971

Each era finds an improvement in law for the benefit of mankind.
—inscribed on Gideon's tombstone,
words that he'd written to his lawyer

You are entitled to a lawyer—whether you are young or old, poor or rich, innocent or guilty, ignorant or educated, nervous or calm. For the American legal system to work, everyone deserves a defense—the disadvantaged need the same protection as the rich and powerful who have so much working in their favor. In a way they need it *more*.

Those who can't pay, however, are typically assigned a government-sponsored public defender, who may be overworked and have scarce resources. In some cases lawyers have time for only one brief meeting with their clients, a half hour before their court appearance. Criminal justice money from the government is limited. Defending suspects might take a lower priority to building more prisons, increasing police protection, and hiring more prosecutors.

Thus the question of whether free counsel is effective counsel is still open. Some believe that the poor are still tremendously disadvantaged at court.

When Is a Minor Not a Minor?

In 1995, a fourteen-year-old boy named Tony Hicks made history. He became the youngest person ever to face the adult punishment for murder in the state of California.

Tony was charged with first-degree murder in the shooting of a pizza deliveryman. Instead of being tried in juvenile court, where he would face ten years in an institution for juvenile offenders, the judge ordered that Tony be tried as an adult—and face the possibility of twenty-five years to life in state prison. California laws had just been changed to allow fourteen- and fifteen-year-olds accused of murder and certain other serious crimes to be tried as adults. Several other states have passed similar laws.

Why is this happening? After all, Tony was technically a minor. Minors are young people under the age of sixteen, seventeen, or eighteen, depending on which state they live in. Minors tend not to have the same rights as adults, nor do they get the same punishments.

Normally, crimes committed by minors tend to be less serious than murder; it is estimated that two-thirds of all burglaries, cases of arson, and robberies are committed by minors. Instead of being handled through the regular justice system, the accused go through juvenile court, which is a special court for minors. After arrest, instead of being held in jail, they are generally released into the custody of their parents, a guardian, or probation officer. If convicted of a crime, they can be sentenced to time in a juvenile prison, sent to an education or rehabilitation program, or released with certain restrictions over a probation period. Some typical probation terms are:

- informing parents of whereabouts at all times
- making restitution to the victim
- attending school
- obeying a curfew, such as being home between ten p.m. and six a.m.
- not participating in a gang
- having no contact with anyone involved with drugs or alcohol

The idea is to change the kid's behavior, to help him or her learn acceptable ways of dealing with life.

Rehabilitation, not punishment.

With young people accused of nonviolent crimes, at least thirty-five states have moved toward the use of teen courts or youth courts—composed of an adult judge and a jury of six to twelve teens. Teen courts provide an alternative less harsh than juvenile court. Sentences may consist of community service work, writing letters of apology, cleaning up graffiti, and counseling. Offenders in teen courts typically have a re-arrest rate less than half of regular juvenile court cases. (For more information: National Association of Youth Courts, **www.youthcourt.net**)

Teen courts are becoming popular in some states.

But young people do commit serious crimes. School shootings and murders committed by young people have shocked many states into lowering the age that juveniles can be tried as adults. The trend now is for children to get adult-type rights under the Bill of Rights—but also adult-type punishments.

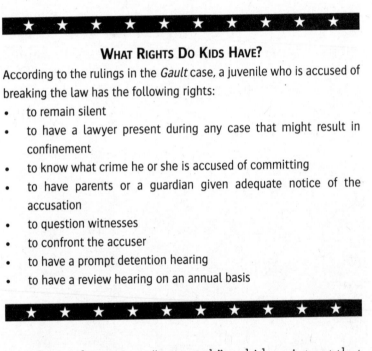

WHAT RIGHTS DO KIDS HAVE?

According to the rulings in the *Gault* case, a juvenile who is accused of breaking the law has the following rights:

- to remain silent
- to have a lawyer present during any case that might result in confinement
- to know what crime he or she is accused of committing
- to have parents or a guardian given adequate notice of the accusation
- to question witnesses
- to confront the accuser
- to have a prompt detention hearing
- to have a review hearing on an annual basis

Those who want to "get tough" on kids point out that special protection for kids is a relatively new concept in this country. Children in the early days of the United States were tried as adults, served sometimes long prison terms in the same jails as adults, and were even in some cases tortured or executed. Over the years, the courts have lightened up a bit on kids, aiming for rehabilitation rather than punishment, but kids were still denied basic rights—like a lawyer—until 1967 and *In re Gault*.

Now the pendulum of juvenile justice is swinging back toward the harsher old days. The focus now is protecting society by putting young criminals out of sight. Kids who commit crimes with the thought that "I'm a juvenile—the courts can't really do anything to me" are finding out that the reality is different: they *will* be held accountable for what they do.

Offenders younger than ten still do tend to be held not legally accountable for their actions. Rather than being made to pay a price, they may be sent to a training school or turned over to some sheltered setting in an effort at rehabilitation. But with older children, society is calling for punishment, not just attempts at rehabilitation.

More on Justice for Young People

State laws regarding juvenile justice vary widely— there is no one system. This is a changing area, and it's of vital interest to kids, partly because of the trend toward harsher treatment of kids, but also because many kids are themselves victims of youthful criminals.

AND WHAT ABOUT CURFEWS?

As part of society's "get tough" policy on youthful crime, many cities are simply requiring kids to stay home, for their own protection as well as society's. In recent years, hundreds of cities have passed or strengthened curfews requiring minors to be off the streets after ten p.m. When curfew laws are aggressively enforced, kids who violate them, whether or not they have a legitimate reason to be out and about, can be arrested, photographed, and fingerprinted as would be any other person suspected of a crime.

Many cities impose curfews to try to get kids to stay at home.

But are juvenile curfews constitutional? Don't they violate the rights of *all* minors, not just the ones involved in criminal activity? So far the state courts have disagreed, and the Supreme Court has yet to rule. In 1994 it rejected a challenge to the curfew law in Dallas, which suggests that it does find curfews constitutional.

Meanwhile, check the law in your state.

In spite of all this, you may have noticed that the Sixth Amendment says nothing special about the rights of juveniles. Kids do tend to get lost in the shuffle during talk of criminal justice. When Gerald Gault's case got to the Supreme Court, it was only the second time in its history that the Court reviewed a case involving a minor.

In essence, kids do not always have the right to trial by jury, but they do have most of the other rights of the accused. In other words, sometimes the protections of the Sixth Amendment apply to them, and sometimes they don't. They were more likely *not* to before *In re Gault*.

(For more, visit National Center for Juvenile Justice, **www.ncjj.org**)

A Shelter for Criminals?

Once again, *Gault* and other landmark cases, such as the *Miranda* case, were not meant to make it impossible for police to solve crimes. A gap exists between those who criticize the Bill of Rights as "soft on crime" and those who respect it and take it seriously. People who argue for more "law and order" sometimes see the Sixth

Amendment as a shelter for criminals.

But by protecting the right to a lawyer and other rights, the Amendment instead offers a shelter for those who:

- have been falsely accused
- confess because they have been tricked or confused
- are poor or young or otherwise at a disadvantage

The Sixth is meant as a step toward making sure that the United States offers "liberty and justice for all," not just liberty and justice for the wealthy.

And with the Bill of Rights and this Amendment, the United States became the first country in the world to provide this sort of protection for its citizens.

CHAPTER 10

The Seventh Amendment, or Civil Justice

★ ★ ★

In Suits at common law, where the value in controversy shall exceed twenty dollars, the right of trial by jury shall be preserved, and no fact tried by jury shall be otherwise re-examined in any Court of the United States, than according to the rules of the common law.

You do have to wait until you're eighteen to serve on a jury, but after that almost everyone gets summoned. Indeed, if there were a prize for the Amendment most likely to affect average Americans, it would go to the Seventh. Most of us may never house a soldier, commit a crime, be searched or seized, or take the Fifth. But sooner or later everyone gets called for jury duty.

A Twenty-Dollar Value

With the Seventh Amendment we move away from criminal law—the Fifth and Sixth Amendments wrapped up that topic. This one refers to noncriminal, or civil, cases. The people's rights are preserved in these trials, too, according to the Seventh Amendment. All citizens have the right to trial by jury in cases where they go to court to settle disputes about money or property.

But twenty dollars?

Originally, a jury trial was guaranteed when the amount in question surpassed twenty dollars—equivalent to about forty days' wages in 1791. This was supposed to rule out the less important cases, which a judge could handle alone. Today, in federal civil cases, lawsuits between citizens of different states must involve $75,000. For lawsuits within a state, the required amount varies from state to state.

This inflation is a major sign of the times, like so much else about the way the Bill of Rights is interpreted now.

Life Without a Seventh Amendment

The concept of a jury of one's peers is so beloved in the United States that it's worth asking why. It turns out that American society would be vastly different without this protection.

★ ★ ★ ★ ★ ★ ★ ★ ★ ★

CONSIDER THE ALTERNATIVES

Here are some of the ways disputes were settled before the Seventh Amendment:

- The blood feud, prevalent in early English history: If someone hurt or killed a member of a family, that family took revenge by hurting or killing someone from the killer's family. Then that family would take revenge, and so on. This cycle would last for years, until there was no one to remember the original cause.

- The hue and cry, from the same period: A villager went about town crying out (truthfully or not) that someone had wronged him. People of the village got together, found the accused person, and killed him or her on the spot.

- The cold-water ordeal: In old English law, accused people were tied up, then thrown into a river. If they floated, they were guilty. If they drowned, they were innocent (though dead).

- Ordeal by fire: Wealthier accused people in thirteenth-century

England would have to walk barefoot and blindfolded over red-hot pieces of iron. If their wounds healed quickly, they were innocent.

The unhealthy "ordeal by fire" in England of the Middle Ages.

- Oath-repeating: Twelve of your friends would have to swear you were innocent, repeating a complex oath many times. If any of them made a mistake, it was considered a sign that you were guilty.
- Trial by battle: The accused would fight the accuser with fists or axes. They believed that God would spare the one who was telling the truth. (You could hire someone to do your fighting for you.)
- One judge listened to all the evidence and settled all disputes, often according to whim or his own interests.

★ ★ ★ ★ ★ ★ ★ ★ ★ ★

Of all the nasty possibilities, it was the idea of one judge making all judgments that most struck fear into supporters of the Seventh Amendment. A judge could be corrupt and open to bribes, or wealthy and likely to side with his wealthy friends.

Considering the alternatives, it's no wonder that the right to trial by jury was a cause worth fighting the American Revolution for. It became a symbol of the people's right to govern themselves. Some even saw the right to trials by juries as more important than the right to make laws. More than 90 percent of all jury trials in the world are now held in the United States.

Types of Civil Trials
The common image of a trial implies a crime. But there are plenty of other reasons why people go to court. For various reasons, noncriminal cases are increasing.

These are just some of the endless number of disputes that come before a civil jury:
• people injured in accidents who can't agree with their insurance companies on a fair settlement
• people who sue a restaurant for serving coffee that's too hot and burns them
• property owners who sue tenants for rent owed
• patients who sue a doctor for malpractice—possible mistakes in medical treatment
• people who have been badly injured by unsafe products, and sue the manufacturers for injuries caused by these products
• victims of identity theft who sue the thief
• arguments over land—who owns what
• workers who sue employers for injuries caused by unsafe conditions on the job

Civil trials often involve injured people.

• people who sue for libel, that is, for publishing information that damages their reputation
• people suing companies that made their buildings with asbestos, a material now known to cause cancer
• smokers who sue cigarette companies claiming that their products caused ill health or death
• minorities who have been discriminated against by business or government
• families contesting a dead person's will
• neighborhood disputes
• victims of companies whose computers have been hacked, revealing their personal information

Many factors go into deciding the amount to be awarded to the winner of a civil case—the customs of a community, the amount of pain and suffering involved, the emotions and sympathies of the jury, the extent of the defendant's bad conduct, the wish to set an example for other wrongdoers. The amount of the settlements can range from token sums to incredible amounts—millions of dollars. These high settlements are controversial, and some people call for arbitrary limits to be set.

Who's Who on the Jury

A jury is a nifty concept—a "twelve-heads-are-better-than-one" idea. It is meant to provide a variety of perspectives with which to sort out the evidence presented in court and arrive at the truth.

But it's been a struggle throughout American history to make juries truly representative of the population. Important Supreme Court cases that have served to create balanced juries include:

• *Strauder v. West Virginia* (1880)—Taylor Strauder, an African American, had been tried for murder by an all-white jury. The Supreme Court ruled in his favor, holding that for a trial to be fair, whole racial groups couldn't be excluded from the jury. Nevertheless, blacks continued to be unfairly and illegally excluded from juries for many years.

• *Thiel v. Southern Pacific Company* (1946)—The Supreme Court ruled that a jury does not have to have "one of everything" in the community, but that no one can be deliberately excluded from a jury on the basis of race, religion, beliefs, or income.

• *Hernandez v. Texas* (1954)—The conviction of a

Mexican American was reversed because no one with a Hispanic name had served on a jury in that county for twenty-five years.

• *Taylor v. Louisiana* (1975)—The Supreme Court finally ruled that the "fair cross-section requirement" for a jury trial was "violated by the systematic exclusion of women."

Today the court system works hard to find all types of people—young and old, rich and poor, from different ethnic groups, and holding various types of jobs.

Jurors are typically ordinary citizens, not necessarily scholars or experts. But what happens when cases are exceedingly complex? A jury trial can seem an odd method of getting at the truth. Unwieldy cases or those with lots of technical jargon can take years. The boredom and frustration can put a strain on jurors' daily lives, not to mention their brains.

★ ★ ★ ★ ★ ★ ★ ★ ★ ★ ★ ★ ★ ★

It borders on cruelty to draft people to sit for long periods trying to cope with issues largely beyond their grasp.
—Warren E. Burger, Supreme Court Justice 1969–1986

★ ★ ★ ★ ★ ★ ★ ★ ★ ★ ★ ★ ★ ★

The courts have not yet come to agreement on this issue. Some judges argue that a judge alone, or a panel of experts, should decide certain cases; having a regular jury makes a complex trial unfair.

Others believe that no case is too difficult for ordinary people; the jury's most important job is to decide who is telling the truth, and common sense is its primary tool. Meddling with juries seems a betrayal of the Seventh Amendment.

A Magic Number

And why twelve people? No one really knows. The number is not in the Constitution or Bill of Rights. The Supreme Court has even ruled that twelve people are not particularly required for a jury—six would be okay, too. Twelve seems to be a nice round number, just a custom, perhaps deriving from the number of apostles in the Bible or the tribes of Israel.

No matter what controversies continue to swirl around the Seventh Amendment, only a minority of Americans have suggested doing away with it. Most would agree: Twelve people using their common sense sounds a lot better than being tossed into icy water or forced to walk barefoot over hot pieces of iron.

CHAPTER 11

The Eighth Amendment, or Punishments

★ ★ ★

Excessive bail shall not be required,
nor excessive fines imposed, nor cruel
and unusual punishments inflicted.

One day in Florida, an African American boy named James Ingraham and another student received a severe paddling at their school. A teacher hit James more than twenty times as he was being held down on a table.

What does "cruel and unusual" mean to you? For many kids, it refers to cases like James's, when school officials punish students in a physical way. Do students have protection under the Bill of Rights—is paddling another form of child abuse?

This question of physical, or corporal, punishment in the public schools is a flaming issue related to the Eighth Amendment. Some cities have banned corporal punishment, and many national groups—such as the Parent-Teacher Association, the American Medical Association, and the American Bar Association—have condemned the practice.

So far, though, the Supreme Court has ruled that corporal punishment is not cruel and unusual under the Eighth Amendment. In James's case (*Ingraham v. Wright*, 1977), the Court concluded that physical punishment is acceptable as long as it is reasonably necessary for the proper education and discipline of a student. Advance notice or a hearing for the student to be heard is not required *before* punishment. All students have is the right to sue *afterward*, under the Eighth Amendment, if the punishment is excessive or if it is used in a racially discriminatory manner; but to receive compensation, the student has to prove that the punishment was not justified.

This ruling made it clear that the Eighth Amendment applies only to adults (criminal adults, that is), not to children. "Supervision by the community," as the Court put it, is supposed to safeguard young people from the type of abuse that the Eighth Amendment protects adults from.

Ingraham v. Wright does not prevent states or school districts from banning corporal punishment. Currently, though, nineteen states do allow paddling and hitting of students by teachers. It is most common in the South, especially in Texas and Arkansas. Bills have been introduced in Congress to end corporal punishment, but most officials seem to feel that this is an issue for local schools to handle, not the government. Kids and adults who think that getting hit by teachers is degrading, not to mention cruel and unusual, need to speak up.

MORE INFORMATION ON STUDENT PUNISHMENTS

For resources on the rights of students and parents in this area, contact:

- National Youth Rights Organization, **www.youthrights.org**
- Global Initiative to End Corporal Punishment of All Children, **www.endcorporalpunishment.org**
- American Civil Liberties Union, Corporal Punishments in Schools, **www.aclu.org/blog/tag/corporal-punishments-schools**

"Excessive Bail"

In general, the Eighth Amendment speaks to adults, but the topics are intriguing. It wraps up—for now—the whole subject of people's rights in the judicial system. It deals with the conclusion of the crime-and-punishment process: the punishment part.

What does bail have to do with this? If those accused of a crime are considered trustworthy, they are allowed to be responsible for themselves: they promise to be in court at the required time and are released on what is called "their own recognizance." In most states, juveniles are automatically released into the custody of their parents.

But if there is a question about whether defendants will try to escape, they must post, or come up with, bail. Bail is not exactly punishment. It's an amount of money that a person accused of a crime must pay in order to stay out of jail until the jury comes to a verdict. Since people are presumed innocent until proven guilty, part of the purpose of bail is to prevent injustice. A possibly innocent person should not have to await trial from a jail cell.

Bail can be paid by the accused or by somebody else who is willing to trust him or her. After the trial, the money gets returned. So the purpose of bail is to guarantee that defendants actually show up for their own trials. In general, the more serious the crime, the higher the bail. Judges set the amount of the bail, and according to this Amendment, they can't set it so high that defendants have no choice but to stay in jail. Demanding a harsh and excessive bail has the same effect as denying bail.

Denying bail is a judgment reserved for those who have proven themselves to be a danger to the community. These people must await their trial in jail.

"Excessive Fines"
When a person has been convicted of a minor violation of the law, the punishment may come in the form of a fine, or a required money payment. Fines are supposed to be fair—they're usually not intended to bankrupt people. Lower courts traditionally establish the fines, and they vary from community to community.

Drunk driving, for example, is generally punished in the United States with a substantial fine (and sometimes a jail sentence). Other countries' penalties for the same offense can be much more excessive:

- In El Salvador, the first offense can be punished with execution by firing squad.
- In Russia, the driver's license can be taken away for life.
- In Malaysia, the driver goes to jail, and if he's married his wife goes to jail, too.
- In South Africa, there is a ten-year prison sentence and/or a $10,000 fine.
- In Bulgaria, the second offense can lead to execution.

In this country, "excessive" has never truly been defined and is frequently controversial. Except for one case—a 1998 ruling that the $357,000 fine for a man failing to report the sum as he left the country was indeed excessive—the Supreme Court has had little to say about it.

"Cruel and Unusual Punishments"

When convicted of serious crimes, people are not supposed to be subjected to cruel and unusual punishment. *This* is the hottest item in the Eighth Amendment—the part that causes the most debate.

Throughout history, horribly painful punishments have been used all around the world. Criminals have been thrown to the lions, mutilated according to the "eye for an eye" principle, crucified, stoned to death, and dismembered.

Early American punishments ranged from fatal to merely embarrassing.

In the New World of the 1780s, the Eighth Amendment would have protected you from being quartered (cut into four pieces), burned at the stake, publicly whipped, branded with a hot iron, or relieved of your ears. A handbook written by an English legal scholar at the time recommended beheading and disemboweling for serious crimes, and the slitting of nostrils for minor crimes.

So the minds behind the Bill of Rights were concerned with the common use of physical torture. This is what they took "cruel and unusual" to mean. But since they didn't define it, the phrase has become ambiguous over the centuries. The meaning of cruel and unusual punishment has become a reflection of the times.

PUNISHMENTS ELSEWHERE

Outside the United States, many countries without a Bill of Rights still use punishments that would be considered cruel, unusual, and barbaric here:

- In North Korea, public torture and executions of political prisoners is common. Prisoners who refuse to renounce their Christian faith can have molten iron poured over them.
- In Brunei, the punishments for rape, adultery, and homosexuality are public whipping, dismemberment, or death by stoning.
- In several Muslim countries governed by strict Sharia law, punishment for theft is amputation of one or both hands.
- In Russia, those arrested for a wide range of crimes are routinely tortured and raped.
- In at least two countries (Saudi Arabia and Iran), punishments include being blinded.
- In Singapore, flogging with a cane is the punishment for vandalism, overstaying a tourist visa, and other crimes.
- In Saudi Arabia, some one hundred people a year are publicly beheaded with a sword.

The most frequent sentence for serious crimes in the United States is jail. Conditions in jail can range from tolerable to horrible, but no one thinks of it as a pleasant experience. It deprives you of your liberty.

Recently, however, many have come to feel that depriving liberty to any but the most violent criminals may be inappropriate punishment. In 2013, with over one and a half million people behind bars, the United States is the world leader in imprisonment (the runners-up were South Africa and Russia). With 5 percent of the world's population, we have 25 percent of its prisoners—an 800 percent increase in the last thirty years. And some of them are juveniles—2,500 of them serving life sentences—in the only country that sentences kids to life imprisonment.

Prisons are massively overcrowded. Some argue that they should be the punishment of last resort, reserved for only the most dangerous criminals. Alternative punishments and treatments could be devised for the majority of criminals, and more could be done to focus on conditions that prevent crime.

Nevertheless, the trend in American justice is to impose stiffer and stiffer jail sentences for a wide variety of crimes. Proposals such as "three strikes, you're out" laws (which impose a mandatory life sentence without parole for the third conviction) are a response to Americans' fear of crime. Some find such laws too harsh. But in 2003 the Supreme Court ruled that they do not violate the Eighth Amendment. Today more than half of the states have some form of a "three strikes, you're out" law.

INFORMATION ON HUMAN RIGHTS ABUSES

The human rights organization Amnesty International was founded to prevent government abuse of fundamental rights. One of its functions is to investigate and stop cruel punishments around the world, most of which would be otherwise kept secret. For more information:

- Amnesty International USA, **www.amnestyusa.org**
- Human Rights Watch, **www.hrw.org**

The Ultimate Punishment

Today the fiercest debate about "cruel and unusual" punishment involves the death sentence. The death penalty, or capital punishment, is generally reserved for murder cases, and it has become the greatest challenge to the Eighth Amendment. Taking a human being's life is the ultimate punishment. Currently, thirty-two states allow the death penalty.

Slow death *would* constitute cruel and unusual punishment, so American methods are intended to be quick:

- two states allow execution by hanging
- three states use the gas chamber
- two states (Oklahoma and Utah) still use a firing squad

The death penalty—the ultimate punishment.

- the others use the electric chair or the lethal injection of a heart-stopping chemical

Any of these methods can cause pain, as "humane" as they may be intended to be. But is execution itself a cruel and unusual punishment?

It *seems* only common sense that someone who cold-bloodedly kills another human being deserves to die. Society is protected—the one executed will never harm anyone again. Knowing that the price will be so steep should prevent others from committing murder. The cost to society should be lower than that of housing murderers in prison for the rest of their lives. Finally, execution appeases the outrage and desire for revenge that many people feel toward those convicted of horrible crimes.

According to the most recent surveys, some 60 percent of Americans (down from 80 percent in 1994) support use of the death penalty and therefore do *not* see it as cruel and unusual. Supporters point out that execution was common during the time the Bill of Rights was written. If Madison and the others had wanted to get rid of it, they would have spelled it out.

Yet opposition to the death penalty is currently on the rise, for all sorts of reasons—religious, moral, practical. Many feel that it is degrading to human dignity to kill anyone deliberately, even those who have committed murder. Times have changed since the Bill of Rights was written—we are now more enlightened about slavery, the equality of women, and so forth—and some now feel that the death penalty has come to represent "legalized homicide."

Numerous countries (including most Western democracies, Mexico, and Canada) have abolished the death penalty. Those that still have it include China, North Korea, Afghanistan, Somalia, Libya, and Guatemala.

★ ★ ★ ★ ★ ★ ★ ★ ★ ★ ★

MORE ON THE ULTIMATE PUNISHMENT

Some of the many places with more information:

- National Coalition to Abolish the Death Penalty, **www.ncadp.org**
- Death Penalty Information Center, **www.deathpenaltyinfo.org**
- Pro-Death Penalty, **www.prodeathpenalty.com**
- Murder Victims' Families for Human Rights, **www.mvfhr.org**
- American Civil Liberties Union, Capital Punishment, **www.aclu. org/capital-punishment**

★ ★ ★ ★ ★ ★ ★ ★ ★ ★ ★

Many dread the finality of the death penalty, the thought that it can't be reversed. What about those accused who turn out to be innocent after all? With new technologies like DNA evidence, we are learning about more and more people who have been put to death who were later proven to be innocent. Lawyers are striving to rescue others. According to the Innocence Project (**www.innocenceproject.org**), more than 300 prisoners have been freed—eighteen of them from death row— since 1989. New DNA evidence caused their convictions to be reversed or thrown out. In 2014, for example, an African American mentally disabled man was declared innocent of a 1983 rape and murder—after spending thirty years on death row. Everyone in the courtroom stood up and cheered.

Imposing such an irreversible penalty goes contrary to the emphasis given in the Bill of Rights toward protecting the innocent.

Some point out that states that execute the most people also tend to have the highest murder rates. This does seem to cast doubt on the idea of execution as a preventative measure. Others argue that capital punishment actually increases the murder rate—it may tempt unbalanced people who want to achieve fame by committing crimes and being executed.

THE PRICE OF A DEATH PENALTY

Those condemned to die are legally allowed to appeal their sentence until they exhaust all possibilities to have it reversed. Courts try to make an effort to make sure an innocent person is not executed. This appeal and review process can take years and cost a great deal of money that the government is constitutionally obligated to pay.

Studies in many states have revealed a significant difference in cost between death penalty cases and life-in-prison cases. The average cost to try and execute a murderer was four to eight times higher—due to the numerous extra steps in the appeals process—than the average cost to try a murder case and keep the convicted person in prison. Costs can run into the millions of dollars, just as all states are trying to cut their budgets.

More people are noticing that the death penalty has been applied in a discriminatory way—against the poor, minorities, and the mentally retarded. Studies show that those who murdered whites were as much as four times more likely to be sentenced to death than those who murdered nonwhites. About 70 percent of those freed from death row so far are people of color. This works strongly against other Bill of Rights provisions that protect against discrimination.

What does the Supreme Court say? So far, most of their decisions have seen capital punishment as constitutional, except in certain cases.

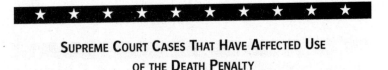

SUPREME COURT CASES THAT HAVE AFFECTED USE
OF THE DEATH PENALTY

- *Furman v. Georgia* (1972) ruled that the death penalty was unconstitutional. This had the effect of halting executions on the basis that laws were being applied in an "arbitrary and capricious" manner (against the poor and minorities), thus violating the prohibition against cruel and unusual punishment.
- *Gregg v. Georgia* (1976) reinstated the death penalty. This allowed executions to be resumed as long as the sentence was not "wantonly and freakishly" imposed.
- *Roberts v. Louisiana* (1976) ruled that laws requiring the death penalty in all murder cases are unconstitutional. Without consideration of "mitigating circumstances" this would be cruel and unusual punishment.
- *Ford v. Wainwright* (1986) ruled that criminals who become and remain insane while on death row cannot be executed.
- *Atkins v. Virginia* (2002) reversed earlier decisions and ruled that executing mentally retarded individuals violates the Eighth Amendment.

What about young people and the death penalty? Can teen murderers be executed? Court decisions have been inclined to say yes. Not until 2005, with *Roper v. Simmons*, did the Supreme Court finally rule it unconstitutional to impose capital punishment for crimes committed while under the age of eighteen (but still constitutional for those over that age). The decision brought the United States in line with the rest of the developed world. Today only Iran, Saudi Arabia, and Sudan are known to execute juveniles.

Opinions on both sides of this issue are passionate. Stay tuned for continued emotional debate.

CHAPTER 12

The Ninth Amendment, or Everything Else

★ ★ ★

The enumeration in the Constitution, of certain rights, shall not be construed to deny or disparage others retained by the people.

What on earth does this sentence mean?

The short answer is that any rights not spelled out in the first eight Amendments belong to the people, not the government. The long answer is more complex—and more interesting.

A Most Mysterious Amendment

In the very beginning of Bill of Rights history, some people opposed the whole thing out of fear. They were paranoid that if the document listed (or enumerated) certain rights that belong to the people—*and not all other possible rights*—then only the listed ones would be protected. Much better to not list any at all—then there would be nothing for the government to take away!

★ ★ ★ ★ ★ ★ ★ ★ ★ ★ ★ ★ ★ ★ ★ ★

THE FATHER OF THE BILL OF RIGHTS RESPONDS TO THE TIMID PEOPLE
This is one of the most plausible arguments I have ever heard urged against the admission of a bill of rights into this system; but, I conceive, that it may be guarded against. I have attempted it, as gentlemen may see.

—James Madison, by way of proposing the Ninth Amendment

★ ★ ★ ★ ★ ★ ★ ★ ★ ★ ★ ★ ★ ★ ★ ★

Now, what are they?

Here is where things get mysterious. And it seems that Madison planned it that way. From what we know, he intended the Ninth Amendment to be *purposely* vague. Its meaning was for the future to decide. At the time it was just one more way to emphasize that the powers of the government were limited.

Uncharted Waters

For a long time, the "future" didn't quite know what to do with this Amendment. Nor did the Supreme Court. Between 1791 and 1965, it mentioned the Ninth only seven times. There was so little activity on it that it became something of an "in-joke" among justices. Actually, as one justice put it, the Court was accomplishing "the seemingly impossible feat of leaving this area of the law more confused than it found it."

The Ninth Amendment rights which are not to be disturbed by the Federal Government are still a mystery to me.
—Robert Jackson, Supreme Court Justice 1941–1954

In its whole existence, a majority of the Court has never ruled that the Ninth provides the sole support for a particular right—it has only been used together with *other* Amendments. But some of the rights not specifically listed in the Constitution are very closely related to rights that are. These would include:

- freedom of association (hanging around with whomever you want)
- the right to vote

The right to vote could fall under the Ninth Amendment.

- the right to be considered innocent until proven guilty
- the right of students to study foreign languages
- the freedom to travel where you want

In these areas the Supreme Court has tended, without much controversy, toward protection.

After 1965, the Court began venturing more boldly into the uncharted waters of the Ninth. So did lower courts—since the 1960s this Amendment has been used in well over 1,000 state and federal court cases.

Some cases that have involved the Ninth Amendment move outside the Constitution and into new topics:

• the right to a clean environment
• the right to an education (in 1973 the Supreme Court ruled that the Constitution did not guarantee this)
• the right to a job
• the right to adequate housing (for those concerned about homelessness)
• the right to bring up your children as you wish
• the freedom to choose your own friendships
• the freedom to wear long hair (for boys in school)
• the right of mothers who give up babies for adoption to keep records sealed
• the right to privacy in same-sex relationships (in 1986 the Supreme Court ruled that this was not protected, meaning that gays and lesbians can be discriminated against)

The right of boys to wear long hair could fall under this Amendment.

• the right to commit suicide, whether or not assisted by a doctor

Though the Supreme Court has ruled on some of these rights, the final word on most of them is probably yet to come.

The Landmark Ninth Amendment Case
So what happened in 1965? This is when the Court

decided the case of *Griswold v. Connecticut.*

Estelle Griswold was the head of the Connecticut branch of Planned Parenthood, a national organization devoted to family planning. Soon after opening a clinic for pregnant women, she was arrested for giving birth control information and instructions to a married couple. It turned out that there was an old law in her state that made it illegal to use birth control devices (contraceptives) or give information about their use.

She was convicted on charges of breaking this law, and her case eventually ended up in the Supreme Court. Her lawyer chose to argue that Connecticut's law was unconstitutional—it violated the right to privacy as guaranteed in part by the Ninth Amendment. The Supreme Court agreed (one justice called the law "uncommonly silly").

According to this ruling, the Constitution protects the right to privacy regarding decisions about having children—for married couples, at least. Such personal decisions were none of the government's business.

So ever since *Griswold*, the Ninth Amendment is usually taken as meaning the right to privacy. This is a big deal.

Other Amendments do seem to support this interpretation. According to the Third, soldiers can't invade the privacy of your home; the Fourth holds that you or your stuff can't be searched except for a good reason. These and other Amendments have what legal scholars call "buffer zones" around them that do imply an attitude of "back off!" that most people have. In one sense the whole Bill of Rights can be taken as a defense of a fundamental right to be left alone.

People in the United States cherish their independence. After 1965, many seized the Ninth Amendment as a nifty tool with which to keep private affairs private. At last, here was specific protection for the right of individuals to pursue their own lives without government meddling.

It should be stressed that not everyone agrees with this interpretation. Some even accuse the Supreme Court of taking on a dangerous sort of power it was never meant to have—inventing rights that do not exist. After all, the word privacy is nowhere in the Constitution, and the Bill of Rights is not supposed to be a bottomless well in which to discover new rights. If Madison had intended that, he could have phrased things differently.

But others argue that this is exactly the Ninth Amendment's purpose—to enumerate new rights as needed and keep the Bill of Rights a living document that changes with the times.

In any case, since *Griswold*, the right to privacy has taken on a life of its own.

And the Most Controversial Ninth Amendment Case

After 1965 arguments about privacy began influencing the debate over illegal abortion—a medical procedure performed for the purpose of ending a pregnancy. Abortion had been legal back in James Madison's day, though unsafe. The movement to ban abortion, which began in the 1850s, was first motivated by its high percentage of fatalities—as many as one-third of women undergoing the procedure died from it. Some people also passionately opposed abortion on moral and religious grounds. Meanwhile, still others maintained that this was a privacy issue—a woman's right to control her own body—that the government had no business interfering with.

In 1973 the Supreme Court's decision in a case called *Roe v. Wade* legalized abortion. The case involved a young Texas woman, Norma McCorvey, who used the name "Jane Roe" in court to protect her from the public spotlight. Pregnant with her second child and already unable to take care of her first, she wanted to end the pregnancy. Abortions were illegal in Texas, and McCorvey's case eventually went before the Supreme Court.

Her lawyers argued that the Texas law violated the right to privacy as established by the interpretation of the Ninth Amendment in *Griswold v. Connecticut*. The Supreme Court ultimately agreed: besides the Ninth, the right to privacy existed under the Fourteenth Amendment (which guarantees equal protection to all citizens—see page 202), and that right did include the right to make one's own decisions about abortion.

This vote created an enormous change in the field of women's health. In particular it has affected the lives of teen girls, the vast majority of whose pregnancies are unplanned, and the amount of control they have over their lives.

But many disagree with the *Roe v. Wade* decision and still feel it was morally wrong on the grounds that abortion is murder. The intense feelings on both sides of this verdict have made it one of the most important cases in Supreme Court history.

Roe v. Wade has, in fact, caused opposition to abortion rights to grow more extreme over the years. There is a strong movement to overturn it, or to invalidate it with restrictive laws that make the procedure extremely difficult to obtain. At least one state has no doctors willing to perform abortions and just one clinic where the doctor flies in from another state. When Texas was scheduled to close all but eight clinics in 2014, the Supreme Court stepped in to temporarily block Texas state law.

Roe v. Wade: by far the most controversial Ninth Amendment case.

Antiabortion, or pro-life, extremists have bombed clinics that perform abortions, and even have murdered doctors who perform them.

SUPREME COURT DECISIONS SINCE *ROE V. WADE*

- By 1989, when its makeup had changed from 1973, the Court seemed to back down from *Roe* with *Webster v. Reproductive Health Services.* This upheld a Missouri law that placed numerous restrictions on abortion. The decision made no mention of the Ninth Amendment. By this time, thirty-one states had passed laws that restricted teen girls' right to an abortion.

- In 1991, with *Rust v. Sullivan* (see page 54, Chapter 3), the Supreme Court upheld a "gag rule" that banned any mention of abortion at federally funded clinics. This decision not only made no mention of the Ninth, but it appears to contradict the First.

- In 1992, with *Planned Parenthood v. Casey*, the Court reaffirmed the right to an abortion but ruled that states could regulate it within reason. This has allowed some states to pass enough laws to make a legal abortion all but impossible. Several states have tried to amend their constitution to ban abortion, or are planning to introduce Amendments to do so.

  Depending on the makeup of the Court, *Roe v. Wade* could still be overturned in the future, making abortion illegal again. So far seven states have passed laws to keep abortion legal if the overturning does take place.

Besides the right to an abortion, the whole subject of personal rights is likely to stay a burning issue. The Ninth Amendment was included in the Bill of Rights to make people feel more secure. And there is no doubt that in years to come it will continue to be quoted for the very same reason.

CHAPTER 13

The Tenth Amendment,
or What About the States?

★ ★ ★

The powers not delegated to the United States by the Constitution, nor prohibited by it to the States, are reserved to the States respectively, or to the people.

In 1916, the United States Congress tried to help out young people. This was a time when many children worked long hours for little money under unhealthy conditions. Congress wanted to end child labor. It decided to ban transportation across state lines of goods made by businesses that employed children under fourteen.

But the states put up an argument. They pointed out that Congress had the power only to regulate commerce *between* states. The power to regulate manufacturing conditions *within* state boundaries was supposed to be reserved to the states.

The Supreme Court, in the end, agreed with the states. In a landmark decision of 1918 (*Hammer v. Dagenhart*), it struck down Congress's well-intentioned Child Labor Law.

This was an example of the Tenth Amendment in action. And people would eventually find other ways to end child labor.

The Oddball Amendment
If you sweat through the language of the Tenth Amendment, you will understand it to say that the government has only the rights spelled out here in the Bill of Rights. The people have the rest.

*   *   *   *   *   *   *   *   *   *   *   *   *

The [Tenth] Amendment states but a truism that all is retained which has not been surrendered.
—Chief Justice Harlan F. Stone, Supreme Court 1925–1946

*   *   *   *   *   *   *   *   *   *   *   *   *

So isn't the Tenth Amendment just a different way of saying the same thing as the Ninth?

Yes, in some ways the Tenth was intended to strengthen the Ninth. It is the final, ultimate, and truly last word on a familiar subject: the power of the federal government (the United States) is limited.

But it's a bit of an oddball, too. It introduces an element that the Bill of Rights has neglected so far: the states. And it shifts from talk about rights to talk about powers.

Federal versus State Government

Each of the fifty states has its own personality, its own quirks. Some states are tiny, some are huge. Some are diverse, some are more homogeneous. Each has its own problems and advantages due to terrain, industries, population, history, weather, levels of income and education, and so on.

The federal government (the one in Washington, DC) deals with the "biggie" problems:

- war and peace
- defending the country
- coining money

- enforcing the Constitution
- establishing foreign policy
- managing trade with foreign countries
- regulating commerce between the states
- providing for the general welfare of the country

But, according to the Tenth Amendment, there are tons of problems that are better off solved closer to home than Washington, DC. State and city governments can be more responsive to the day-to-day lives of their residents. Local solutions to local problems. This is why states can have their own police, for example, and taxes and public education systems.

And, by process of elimination (of what has already been covered by the Bill of Rights), the laws about some topics fall entirely within the states' domain:
- marriage, including same-sex marriage
- divorce
- the right to die
- commerce within the state
- traffic rules
- inheritance laws
- drinking and driving ages
- voting requirements (other than age)
- the ownership, use, and sale of property
- local business laws
- maintenance of roads

According to Madison, the powers of the Washington government are "few and defined." But the powers of the states are "numerous and indefinite." So states are supposed to have the right to run their own affairs without undue interference from Washington.

Some powers represent a seesaw between federal and state governments. Both have a lot to say about crime prevention, for example, criminal justice, the welfare system, abortion rights, and education.

Sometimes power seesaws between federal and state governments.

When a state law conflicts with a federal law, that's a problem. It becomes possible "food" for the Supreme Court to "munch on."

States are not always *right* about their rights. In fact, "states' rights" is a term that at one time meant a rationale for racism, a way for some states to deprive minorities of civil rights guaranteed by the federal government. Amendments had to be added to the Bill of Rights (the Thirteenth, Fourteenth, and Fifteenth—see Chapter 14) in order to prevent this. Over the years, courts have tended to ignore the Tenth for this very reason—it was associated in many people's minds with inappropriate actions by the states.

People who feel that the federal government is getting way too big and intrusive are calling for the Tenth Amendment to be dusted off and put to work more frequently. Some belong to the Tenther Movement, a group maintaining that many of the federal government's actions violate the Tenth Amendment.

In 2014, for example, a Nevada rancher named Cliven Bundy held an armed standoff with police after refusing to pay federal cattle-grazing fees. "I abide by all Nevada state laws," said Bundy, "but I don't recognize the United States government as even existing."

Supreme Court cases related to this Amendment are bound to be coming up.

The way power shifts back and forth between the states and the federal government may sound messy. But it has a huge advantage. It prevents either one from becoming too strong and overpowering individual freedom.

This Amendment sews all the patchwork neatly into a circle: it ends with "the people," the same words that opened the Constitution and the two most frequent words in the Bill of Rights.

CHAPTER 14

There's More?
(Yes—Seventeen Other Amendments)

★ ★ ★

Times change. Wars, terrorist attacks, raised consciousness about social injustices, the ever-increasing pace of new technology, expanded tolerance and knowledge of psychology—all of these and more factors have been hurled at the Bill of Rights.

Luckily, there is a procedure by which new Amendments can be added to the Constitution. It's not easy—it can take up to ten years. Amendments must be:

- proposed in Congress,
- formally passed by Congress,
- sent to the states for approval, and
- approved, or ratified, by three-fourths of the states (this is the part that can take as long as ten years).

Since 1791, a whopping twelve thousand new Amendments have been proposed in Congress, on everything from forbidding duels to prohibiting work by persons under eighteen. But only a tiny percentage—seventeen—have made it all the way through to be ratified.

- #11 (1798) limited the powers of federal courts and kept a state from being sued by citizens of another state. Not considered a terribly significant Amendment today.
- #12 (1804) set procedures for the election of the president and vice president.
- #13 (1865) abolished the slavery of African Americans. Abraham Lincoln's Emancipation Proclamation

in 1863 had not been enough, because Southern states ignored it. This Amendment and the next two corrected a fatal flaw in the original Bill of Rights. Up till now, people were protected against the *federal* government only— the *states* were still free to violate rights (unless forbidden to by their own state constitutions). Madison had wanted this protection from the begin-

Amendment Thirteen reinforced
Abraham Lincoln's
Emancipation Proclamation.

ning, but had been voted down. Finally, with these three Amendments (known as the Civil War Amendments), protection against state government was legally enforceable.

• #14 (1868) defined citizenship and guaranteed equal protection (or "due process of law") to all males. This protected the citizenship of the freed slaves and has been used as leverage to give equal protection in many other circumstances. Usually considered the most important Amendment after the original ten, this one began the "rebirth" of the Bill of Rights. After *Brown v. Board of Education* in 1954, when the Supreme Court ruled that racial segregation in the public schools violated the Fourteenth Amendment, this Amendment became known as the basis for the whole civil rights movement. The landmark case of *Roe v. Wade* (see page

187) also used this as its basis. In an important case for young people (*Goss v. Lopez*, 1975), the Supreme Court used this Amendment to say that before a student is suspended for any length of time, he must be given certain rights of due process, such as a notice of the charges against him.

★ ★ ★ ★ ★ ★ ★ ★ ★ ★ ★ ★ ★ ★

Before the Civil War and the Fourteenth Amendment, the United States **were**. *After the Civil War, the United States* **is**.

—American poet Carl Sandburg

★ ★ ★ ★ ★ ★ ★ ★ ★ ★ ★ ★ ★ ★

• #15 (1870) forbade depriving citizens of the right to vote because of their race. This became necessary because states were passing laws that in various ways denied the vote to free blacks.

• #16 (1913) authorized the income tax—people were now taxed according to how much money they made instead of according to the population of the state where they lived.

• #17 (1913) called for direct election of senators by a vote of the people, instead of being elected by state legislatures. This had the effect of making senators more responsible to ordinary people.

• #18 (1919) is the Prohibition Amendment, forbidding the sale or manufacture of alcohol. This has the distinction of being the only Amendment to be later canceled (see #21).

• #19 (1920) granted women the right to vote. This corrected a major oversight in the Constitution and its Amendments.

- #20 (1933) started presidential and congressional terms in January.
- #21 (1933) repealed #18. Prohibition was an experiment that didn't work—people sold and manufactured alcohol anyway.
- #22 (1951) limited presidents to two terms. Those outraged at Franklin D. Roosevelt's *four* terms were behind this Amendment.
- #23 (1961) gave voting rights to residents of Washington, DC.
- #24 (1964) outlawed the payment of taxes as a voting requirement.
- #25 (1967) established rules of succession if the president is unable to complete a term. It resulted from concerns after President John F. Kennedy was assassinated in 1963.
- #26 (1971) lowered the voting age

Amendment Twenty-four banned the payment of taxes as a voting requirement.

from twenty-one to eighteen. This was the result of pressure during the Vietnam War, when many who were fighting in the war and protesting it were still too young to vote. An important Amendment for young people, giving them a wider say in government.

- #27 (1992) prohibited midterm pay raises for members of Congress.

The Amendment that has zoomed closest to joining these twenty-seven was the Equal Rights Amendment (ERA). The Bill of Rights does nothing special to protect the interests of women, and the ERA would have guaranteed rights regardless of gender, outlawing discrimination based on sex. Enormously controversial, it fell three states short of the thirty-eight required for adoption in 1982, the end of its ten-year limit.

What about the future? Some of the most likely Amendments up for discussion and possible ratification include ones that would

• overturn *Roe v. Wade*, specifically banning abortion

• require Congress and the president to balance the federal budget (this is supported, according to surveys, by a majority of Americans)

• allow prayer in public schools (as a specific exception to the First Amendment)

• overturn the much-criticized decision the Supreme Court made in 2010—Citizens United, which ruled that freedom of speech protects corporations making contributions to political campaigns

• legalize marijuana (according to polls, supported by 58 percent of the public)

• end lifetime appointments for Supreme Court justices (according to polls, supported by 70 percent of the public)

• provide stricter gun control

• specifically prohibit flag burning

• provide equal protection for gays and lesbians

• spell out a right to privacy (supported by people who argue that the word is nowhere in the Bill of

Rights and that the Supreme Court has thus far been "inventing" this right)

• allow presidents to serve for one term only, of six years

• give Washington, DC, representation in Congress

• specifically give rights to the victims of crimes

• enhance the role of the states (elaborating on the Tenth Amendment)

• allow certain immigrants to be eligible for the presidency

With all the additions that have been proposed, it is worth stressing that the Bill of Rights itself—the text of the first ten Amendments to the Constitution—has never been altered in its 200+ years. So far, this unique combination of 462 words has stood the test of time.

★ ★ ★ ★ ★ ★ ★ ★ ★ ★ ★ ★ ★

We were the first people in history to found a nation on the basis of individual rights.
—Warren E. Burger, Supreme Court Justice 1969–1986

★ ★ ★ ★ ★ ★ ★ ★ ★ ★ ★ ★ ★

CHAPTER 15

When the Bill of Rights Goes Wrong

★ ★ ★

There are some who see the interests of government as more important than the rights of the people. They can be actively hostile to the Bill of Rights and would just as soon undermine it.

When the Bill of Rights was written, it *was* a radical challenge to the accepted ideas about government at the time. It's no surprise that some still see it as revolutionary.

There are others who think that the Bill of Rights doesn't go far enough. Also, it is not perfect. To take the most glaring examples, it was worded by rich white males and never intended to apply to American Indians, African Americans, or women. For many years afterward, Congress and the Supreme Court approved policies that legalized unequal treatment.

Not until 1924 was citizenship granted to American Indians. Until then, they were considered "aliens" and had no rights here. For many decades, the Bill of Rights offered Indians no protections, and they were forced to abandon their languages and religions. Their land was taken away, and they were required to live on reservations. In 1830, for example, Congress passed the Indian Removal Act, authorizing the forcible removal of Indians from southern states to territory west of the Mississippi River.

Finally, in 1968, the Indian Civil Rights Act extended the protection of the Amendments to Indians. Sometimes tribal authority takes precedence over state or federal laws, however, and even today laws affecting Indians can be ambiguous.

The institution of slavery, alive and well when the Bill of Rights was written, was a nightmarish contradiction to the ideas in it. Over time, the fact that African Americans were totally excluded from citizenship became harder and harder to ignore. Thomas Jefferson wrote that "the abolition of domestic slavery is the great object of desire," but even he had slaves, as did most Founding Fathers. In the struggle between the financial advantages of enslaved labor and the moral view that slavery is wrong, economics won. American leaders believed it was impossible to both abolish slavery and form a strong Union.

This failure to resolve the contradiction between slavery and liberty eventually resulted in the bloody Civil War. Even after the war, when blacks were finally granted citizenship, unfair laws and terrorism by white supremacist groups worked against blacks' having any real protection under the Bill of Rights. Until the civil rights movement of the 1950s and 1960s, racial segregation was perfectly legal and pervaded all aspects of society.

What does the Negro want? His answer is very simple. He wants only what all other Americans want. He wants opportunity to make real what the Declaration of Independence and the Constitution and the Bill of Rights say.
—American educator Mary McLeod Bethune (1944)

Women were second-class citizens for 130 years after the Bill of Rights, thought of as the property of their husbands. Discrimination on the basis of sex was entirely acceptable, and the Supreme Court thus made what we would consider bizarre decisions. In 1873 it ruled that women were meant to be wives and mothers because of their "timidity and delicacy," and therefore were unfit for occupations such as the law. Six years later it upheld state laws that denied the vote to women. Suffrage for women became a public demand after the first American women's rights convention in Seneca Falls, New York, in 1848. But not until 1920 did the Constitution formally acknowledge it. (As of 2015, women outnumber men in America, but are still by far a minority in government.)

Women fought to vote long before the
Nineteenth Amendment passed in 1920.

The Bill of Rights has often left unprotected the rights of gays and lesbians, the mentally and physically disabled, legal and illegal aliens, students, children, and the poor, in some cases up to the present day. Some of those most often denied their rights are the very people least aware that they have them and least able to hire a lawyer to fight for them.

The Bill of Rights also has no provision for victims' rights. Some feel criminals get lots of protection, while their victims have nothing formal that guarantees their rights to receive compensation, to be free from intimidation, to receive counseling if desired, and to be kept informed of the progress of the investigation of the crime against them.

During wartime or when national security seems threatened, our human rights can shrink. One glaring example of this was the establishment of Japanese American internment camps during World War II.

After the 1941 Japanese attack on Pearl Harbor, many Americans were quick to dehumanize the enemy. Intense patriotism and violent anti-Japanese sentiment led to the forced evacuation of 120,000 people of Japanese ancestry, two-thirds of whom were American citizens. The evacuees were housed in bleak, prison-like camps for about a year before being allowed to return to whatever was left of their former lives. To many besides Japanese Americans, the internment camps felt like the wrong thing to do—because they violated numerous Amendments in the Bill of Rights, notably the Fourth, Fifth, and Sixth.

Those who would give up essential liberty to purchase a little temporary safety, deserve neither liberty nor safety.

—Founding Father Ben Franklin

Even during times of undeclared war, when the danger is possibly less than real, individual rights can be put in jeopardy. During the 1950s, the worldwide spread of Communism (a system of government in which all property is held in common) frightened many in the United States. Some, such as Senator Joseph McCarthy from Wisconsin, took advantage of the panic by branding Americans whom he suspected of being Communists as traitors. Such blacklisting ruined many lives and careers, especially in the entertainment world, while the Bill of Rights and the Supreme Court offered no protection.

Civil rights can be seen as less important whenever the word *war* is used. When the "war on drugs" began in the 1970s, some worried that it was a danger to individual liberty. Such tactics as mandatory drug testing in the workplace and various searches and seizures verge on invasion of privacy.

After the terrorist attacks of 9/11, President George W. Bush declared a "war on terror" in order to mobilize an international military response. Civil liberties again seemed secondary, as with the increased spying by the National Security Agency (page 119). Most visible at the time was the rounding up of nearly 800 Muslim and Arab men. Labeled "enemy combatants," often with questionable evidence, they were taken to an American naval base in Guantanamo Bay, Cuba—technically outside the United States where the Bill of Rights applies.

Everything about the prisoners was secret, even their names. They were held indefinitely without being charged, with warrantless wiretaps on their conversations as they tried to contact lawyers, and subjected to abuse. Their treatment definitely works against the provision that the government is supposed to "play fair," as described on pages 130-131 in Chapter 8 on the Fifth Amendment. It appalled human rights organizations and made some Americans uncomfortable.

We have long since made clear that a state of war is not a blank check for the president when it comes to the rights of American citizens.
—Supreme Court Justice Sandra Day O'Connor, 2004

Several cases involving the detainees have reached the Supreme Court, which has tended to rule in their favor. Most recently, *Boumediene v. Bush* (2008) held that fundamental rights afforded by the Constitution extend to the Guantanamo detainees as well. Over the years, most of the men have been released without charges or sent to their home countries. President Barack Obama promised to close the prison, but it remains open, with a dwindling list of aging prisoners.

Greater knowledge of the Bill of Rights could prevent it from going wrong again. With wider visibility—more information online and cameras now widely allowed in courtrooms (though not in the Supreme Court)— probably at no time in history has a wider range of people been aware of what goes on inside a courtroom. Many people are casually and ably discussing legal tidbits only lawyers used to know about.

Will cameras in the courtrooms affect the Bill of Rights?

Meanwhile, the Bill of Rights has had a rich and strange life. It remains a living document, shifting with the times and public opinion. Its goal—to protect our rights and liberties as United States citizens—is not always perfectly reached, and there are some who find it too intrusive.

But most people, especially newly arrived immigrants from other countries, will agree: through the freedoms it protects, the Bill of Rights has contributed toward making the United States unlike any other nation on earth.

Thanks to the 100-pound giant, the United States is unlike any other nation on earth.

★ ★ ★

SOURCES and SUGGESTIONS FOR FURTHER READING

*Material especially for young readers is starred (*).*

Alderman, Ellen, and Caroline Kennedy. *In Our Defense: The Bill of Rights in Action.* New York: Morrow, 1991.

American Civil Liberties Union, **www.aclu.org**

Bill of Rights Defense Committee, **www.bordc.org**

* Bill of Rights Institute, **www.billofrightsinstitute.org**

Bodenhamer, David J., and James W. Ely. *The Bill of Rights in Modern America.* Bloomington, IN: Indiana University Press, 2008.

Center for Constitutional Rights, **www.ccrjustice.org**

First Amendment Center, **www. firstamendmentcenter.org**

* Freedman, Russell. *In Defense of Liberty: The Story of America's Bill of Rights.* New York: Holiday House, 2003.

Glasser, Ira. *Visions of Liberty: The Bill of Rights for All Americans.* New York: Arcade, 1991.

* Graham, Amy. *A Look at the Bill of Rights: Protecting the Rights of Americans*. Berkeley Heights, NJ: Enslow, 2007.

Hentoff, Nat. *The War on the Bill of Rights—and the Gathering Resistance*. New York: Seven Stories Press, 2004.

Library of Congress, Primary Documents in American History, The Bill of Rights, **www.loc.gov/rr/program/bib/ourdocs/billofrights.html**

* McGowen, Tom. *The Great Monkey Trial: Science vs. Fundamentalism in America*. New York: Watts, 1990.

Marsh, Dave. *Fifty Ways to Fight Censorship and Important Facts to Know About the Censors*. New York: Thunder's Mouth Press, 1991.

* Meltzer, Milton. *The Bill of Rights: How We Got It and What It Means*. New York: Crowell, 1990.

National Archives, Bill of Rights, **www.archives.gov/exhibits/charters/bill_of_rights.html**

* Rappaport, Doreen. *Tinker vs. Des Moines: Student Rights on Trial*. New York: HarperCollins, 1993.

* Smith, Rich. *The Bill of Rights: Defining Our Freedoms*. Edina, MN: ABDO, 2007.

* Sobel, Sly. *The Bill of Rights: Protecting Our Freedom Then and Now*. Hauppauge, NY: Barron's, 2008.

* Stein, Conrad R. *The Bill of Rights*. Chicago: Children's Press, 1992.

Stevens, John Paul. *Six Amendments: How and Why We Should Change the Constitution*. New York: Little, Brown, 2014.

Supreme Court, **www.supremecourt.gov**

Supreme Court of the United States Blog, **www.scotusblog.com**

* Teaching American History, Bill of Rights, **www. teachingamericanhistory.org/bor/**

Wagman, Robert J. *The Supreme Court: A Citizen's Guide.* New York: Pharos Books, 1993.

Waldman, Michael. *The Second Amendment: A Biography.* New York: Simon & Schuster, 2014.

* Yero, Judith Lloyd. *The Bill of Rights.* Washington, DC: National Geographic, 2006.

INDEX